To Alisa -

Yeah, yeah - another book :)

But it fit the theme.

Love Ya

Renée

Bob Plager's Tales from the Blues Bench

A Collection of the Greatest
St. Louis Blues Tales Ever Told

Bob Plager
with Tom Wheatley

Sports Publishing L.L.C.
www.sportspublishingllc.com

Director of production: Susan M. Moyer
Project manager: Jim Henehan
Dust jacket design: Kenneth J. O'Brien
Developmental editor: Doug Hoepker
Copy editor: Cindy McNew and Holly Birch

ISBN: 1-58261-747-3

Printed in the United States of America

Sports Publishing L.L.C.
www.sportspublishingllc.com

To my daughter Melissa and my son Bobby, my biggest fans and best friends.

To my father Gus, who taught us to be tough before he passed away, and to my mother Edith, who still worries about me.

To my brother Barc, whom I miss the most, and to his family, who lived up to the Plager name.

To my brother Billy, who was hard to play against and fun to play with, and to his family.

To the Blues Alumni, who are part of our family.

And to all the loyal St. Louis hockey fans, who treated us like family.

—Bob Plager

To my mom, Marge Wheatley, who knows where Primante's is...and a whole lot more.

—Tom Wheatley

Contents

Introduction

To be sitting here writing a book, it all goes back to where I grew up, in a little town in northern Ontario called Kirkland Lake.

As a kid, being a Canadian, there's a dream that you have. You say your prayers and ask God, "Please let me play in the National Hockey League."

But it was a dream. I was born in 1943, and there were only six teams in the NHL when I was growing up.

Kirkland Lake was a gold-mining town. So many hockey players came out of there through the years. Ted Lindsay was the first big star from my town when I was a kid, and then there was Ralph Backstrom.

You wanted to be like them. Everybody in the town played hockey. I came two years after my brother Barclay, and my brother Billy came two years after me. We lived across the road from a rink.

Back then, every rink was outdoors. If it got to be 40 below—we didn't have wind-chill factors—the games were canceled. That didn't bother us. We just went and played pickup games.

Our school had a full-sized rink, 200 feet by 85 feet. It was just a sheet of ice. No boards, just snow banks.

You'd bring your own puck with your name or your initials carved in it. We couldn't afford many pucks, and when you shot one into the snow bank, you'd dig it out and make sure it was yours.

When recess came, you ran down to the rink. Recess was only 15 minutes. You didn't have time to put your skates on. So you played in your boots till the bell rang.

But lunch was an hour. You'd grab your skates and be eating your sandwich on your way downstairs to the rink. They had a rink shack there with a big stove in it. You'd put your skates on in there and go out and play all through the lunch hour.

You went out in your Montreal Canadiens sweater or your Toronto Maple Leafs sweater, because those were the only two Canadian teams in the NHL.

We had no TV. You listened to the radio. On Saturday night—every Saturday night—it was Hockey Night in Canada.

The Canadiens or Maple Leafs would always be on. And you'd dream and you'd pray that some night you might get to play on Hockey Night in Canada.

Years later my brothers and I all played together on the ice at the same time for the St. Louis Blues.

We were in Montreal, and Scotty Bowman sent the three of us out to start the game. Normally we were all defensemen. I remember Scotty saying the lineup in the dressing room: "Barclay Plager, center ice. Bob Plager, left wing. Billy Plager, right wing."

There were seven players from Kirkland Lake who started that game. The Canadiens sent out Ralph Backstrom, Dickie Duff and Mickey Redmond as forwards and Larry Hillman on defense.

You dream and you pray.

I remember a little problem my mother had at our school, after her boys said they were going to be hockey players no matter what. When she let Barclay go away to play junior hockey at 16, the principal said to her, "Your boys will be nothing but hockey bums."

Nothing was said back to the principal. But in my second year, after I went to the Stanley Cup finals for the second time in a row with the Blues, Kirkland Lake was having a big reunion.

All three Plager boys were in the NHL.

I had a brand new '69 Riviera that I drove up for the reunion. Then I had to leave to do a hockey school for a week.

I said, "Mum, I'm leaving the car here. I want you to drive my car every day to the principal's house. Every day when you get there, I want you to beep the horn until the principal comes out.

"And every day when he comes out, just say to him, 'The boys aren't doing too bad in hockey, are they?'"

Tales from the Blues Bench

An Original Blue

I made it to the NHL before either of my brothers. I had played for the New York Rangers, but I had been up and down from the minor leagues in Baltimore for two years.

Then, in 1967 the NHL decided to expand from six teams to 12 teams. The expansion draft was in June. I sat there in Baltimore all day and I wasn't drafted. Afterwards, I rated the draft for the writers. I thought Oakland got the best players from the Original Six teams. I didn't think St. Louis did a very good job. Of the six new teams, I had them in sixth place.

The next day I got called by a writer. He said, "Guess what? The Rangers traded you to St. Louis."

I said, "Nice try. You're not going to get me."

I thought he was pulling my leg.

He said, "No, really. You, Timmy Ecclestone, Gary Sabourin and Gordie Kannegiesser got traded for Rod Seiling."

The Blues had drafted Seiling from the Rangers, who wanted him back.

Then the writer said, "You picked St. Louis as the worst expansion team. What do you have to say about that now?"

I said, "Hockey's a strange sport. It's amazing how with one good trade you can go all the way from last place to first!"

Checking In

That first training camp with the Blues in '67 was at the old St. Louis Arena. It was the worst place to have camp, so hot and humid. I played in the Arena in the minors when I was with St. Paul of the International Hockey League. What an awful building. We used to stickhandle the mice in the dressing room. You'd tip up your skates to put them on, and a mouse would run out. They had cats all over the place to keep the mice down.

When we got to the Arena for training camp in '67, they remodeled the whole place. They were still welding seats so we could play hockey. They turned that old rink into a beautiful place to play.

But we would die in the heat in there. Lynn Patrick was the head coach. Scotty Bowman was the assistant coach, and Cliff Fletcher worked with the team then in camp and was a scout.

We had drafted Glenn Hall, who had been a great goalie, but he didn't show up for camp. He was famous for painting his barn back in Canada every summer. Everybody in hockey knew about Glenn Hall and his red barn. That was his excuse for missing camp.

There were no goalie masks back then. He hated facing pucks anyway, which is why he threw up before every game. But in camp, all the players—especially the kids—tried to impress somebody with their shot. They shot high at the net to show they could go top corner.

So, Glenn was a target. He had to stop thousands of shots in camp. He'd say, "You're getting hit everywhere. After awhile you can't move your shoulder, you can't move your hand, pucks are flying at your head."

He was a Hall of Fame goalie. He felt he didn't need to go through all of that in camp. So he just didn't show up.

Al Arbour didn't either. Not right away. Al was older, too, and he'd won a few Stanley Cups with Toronto and Detroit as a defenseman. I had never played with Al but I'd played against him. He was the kind of guy who didn't have great stats, but teams always traded for him just before the playoffs.

We played our first five exhibition games in five nights. But first we had an intrasquad game in Pekin, Illinois. And it was a bloodbath. There were 40 guys in camp, and they all wanted to show why they should make the team.

Then Al met us in Rochester, New York. He had been with the Rochester Americans, a minor league team, the year before. It looked like his NHL career was over. Because of expansion, he got to play. And I think he played four exhibition games in four nights.

I remember telling Lynn Patrick, "I picked you to finish last because you drafted all these old guys."

I knew Lynn because his brother, Muzz, was the general manager in New York when I was in the Rangers system.

Lynn said, "There were some good players with better statistics that we didn't draft. But look around the dressing room. Everyone has a ring. They've been in championships in the NHL or the minors or juniors.

"They know how to win. And the other guys, those better players we passed up in the draft? Come April, they go home. And the guys we drafted? They keep going in the playoffs."

The Canadien Connection

Those first years in St. Louis, I'd say a third of our team was Montreal Canadiens. Scotty Bowman had coached in the Montreal system. Barclay Plager and Jimmy Roberts had played for Scotty at Peterborough in the finals of the Memorial Cup, the junior championship of Canada. We had Canadiens like Dickie Moore, Jean-Guy Talbot, Red Berenson, Noel Picard, Billy McCreary, Doug Harvey, Phil Goyette, Jacques Plante. Some of these guys had three, four, five Stanley Cups. They were here to teach the younger guys the Montreal tradition—how to win—which they did.

We learned what the Bluenote meant. The sacrifices it took to win. The way you stuck together as a team. When you got on that 200-by-85 foot sheet of ice, winning was the number-one thing. At all costs.

Know When to Say Fun

We went to the Stanley Cup finals in our first three years. We never won the Cup, but no expansion team in any sport ever went to the finals its first three years.

When you look at how we won and what we learned, one lesson was that you can't buy fun. The other was that you pick your spots.

Nobody partied more and had more fun and acted crazier than the guys from Montreal. But when you went over the boards for a game or practice, you were ready. You never let fun get in the way of work.

The other thing was: You were a team. The early Blues went out and had lunch after every practice—17, 18, 19 guys. It was McDermott's today or Rigazzi's tomorrow, but you went as a team. If you didn't drink beer, okay, you had a Coke. But you did it together. If you had family or parents in town to see you, hey, there was a table over there for them. You'd be with them later, but you'd start out with the team.

Because when you have a couple beers together, that's like truth serum if something's bothering you. Maybe one of the younger players was intimidated to talk to the older veterans, but they'd talk after a couple of beers.

You never went out the night before a game. Someone would say on a road trip, "Hey, it's Monday night. When do we play again?" The answer would come back: "Wednesday!"

That meant everybody went out that night. Together. Maybe you all stayed out a little later than you should, but the next day at practice you skated your butt off.

Dickie Moore told us younger guys, "Hey, you're single and it's great to have your fun. But if you go out the night before a game, or if it interferes with how you play, then you're stealing money from me. And nobody, *nobody*, steals money from me!"

You never argued with Dickie Moore. He wasn't big, but he was the meanest, toughest player. He taught you to have pride in your sweater.

One time in Oakland we came off the ice after a game, and one of the players was mad. He threw his sweater on the dressing room floor. I don't remember if we won or lost, but this guy was mad. Dickie Moore grabbed him by the throat and put him up against the wall. The guy's feet were off the floor.

And Dickie Moore said: "That sweater *never* hits the floor. That crest never touched the floor in Montreal. That Bluenote, that crest, is your life. It's your livelihood. You take pride in it."

Young guys like me and Barclay Plager and Timmy Ecclestone and Craig Cameron and Terry Crisp all saw that. We learned to take pride in that sweater. It never hit the floor again in that dressing room.

When Barclay, Noel Picard and myself became veterans, we passed that on to the younger guys like Brian Sutter and Bernie Federko. Nobody wore the Bluenote with more pride than Brian and Bernie. And Barclay taught both of them in the minors when he coached in Kansas City.

Brian Sutter became the captain of the Blues and passed it on to the younger guys who came after him. Now he's the coach in Chicago, and I bet you that sweater never touches the floor up there.

Playing Hurt

Dickie Moore used to cry after every game. There was nothing left in his knee. It was rubbing bone on bone. He eventually had to retire because his knee hurt so bad.

He was the toughest, meanest guy in the world and you'd see tears in his eyes. We didn't have the surgeries and the rehab and the exercise machines that they have now. We had one bicycle for rehab. Actually, I think that was for me to get my weight down every weigh-in!

We all grew up playing with injuries—we *had* to play. There were only 12 teams and 240 jobs. If you sat out with an injury you might not get your spot back. Ever.

Tommy Woodcock was our trainer. If your shoulder was dislocated, he could tape it so it'd never pop out. Same thing if you had sore ribs or a bad knee. If it was the knee, you'd get up on the table and stand on two pucks stacked under your heel. That would flex the knee. Tommy would tape it up and then you'd jump down off the table. You'd land and say, "Okay, Tom, good one!"

That's how you knew your knee wouldn't hurt as much.

Your trainer had to be a good taper. And Tommy Woodcock was the best taper in hockey.

Scotty Takes Charge

S ome people think Scotty Bowman was the first coach of the Blues, but he actually came in as the assistant to Lynn Patrick.

In training camp I made a joke about Scotty, and Lynn said, "You better watch out. He may be your next coach."

And he was. After 26 games, Lynn decided to concentrate on being the general manager, his other job. I think Lynn planned to step aside for Scotty all the time.

Scotty had just turned 34. He was younger than a lot of the players. Dickie Moore and Glenn Hall were 36. Al Arbour was 35. Scotty was so young that the Salomons, our owners, would never have hired him as the head coach at the start. But Lynn knew how good Scotty was.

Scotty didn't try to order the veterans around at the start. He let them help him run the team. If a player wouldn't take a hit, Dickie Moore would say, "Don't worry, Scotty. We'll take care of that."

The next day in practice, the guy would get smashed into the boards.

Scrimmages were a lot different then. You wouldn't let anybody score. A lot of guys got hurt in practice. You played the way you played in the game. Tough.

I didn't play the power play, but I killed penalties. When you killed penalties in practice, you took so much pride in that. You worked, you hit, you got down and blocked shots. They were not going to score on the power play in practice, and that carried over to the games.

At first, Scotty would consult with the older guys at practice. Barclay would argue with him, because they knew each other so well. But my brother was the only one who ever did that. Because Scotty was a little crazy.

The Best One

Scotty took over near the end of November that first year. The next day he said to me, "We just made a trade."

I asked him whom we got. He said, "I got the good one!"

He was all excited. I still had no clue what he was talking about. I said, "Okay, what do you mean?"

He said, "I got the best one."

I said, "Who?"

He said, "I got your brother Barclay."

Scotty didn't have to tell me that Barclay was the best Plager. I already knew that. And I knew that Scotty knew it.

We got Barclay and Red Berenson from the New York Rangers for Ron Attwell and Ron Stewart. The city didn't like that trade. Our two best scorers were traded for Red, who sat the bench in New York, and Barclay, who had never played in the NHL. But, Red was the greatest skater and practice player ever. And so skilled. And everywhere that Scotty went, Barclay went with him. Because Barclay Plager would do *anything* to win a hockey game.

If we were losing to somebody 5 to 1, Scotty would say to Barc, "You have to go out and beat every one of those guys."

And Barc would try to fight every guy out there. That's the way he was growing up, too. I watched him and I learned.

There are a lot of reasons I got to the NHL and played 11 years. And Barclay Plager is the main one.

Scotty on Duty

Scotty was single when he was here. Barc was married when we got him, but his wife Helen had just given birth and stayed back in Canada with the baby. So, Barc stayed with me and Ray Fortin in an apartment on Lindell Boulevard, near the St. Louis Cathedral.

One night we were sitting out front and Scotty drove by. He didn't stop but Barc said, "He's checking up on us."

Scotty went around the block and came by again. Barc ran over and yelled. Scotty stopped and Barc asked him what he was doing.

"The Best One" When Scotty Bowman said that about Barclay, he got no argument from the rest of us Plagers. (*Bruce Bennett Studios*)

Scotty said, "I've got this French newspaper, and I thought maybe Ray wanted to read it."

That was his explanation of why he came all the way over to our place at night. We figured he probably wanted to see if our car was there or if we were out. So, after that, we started parking the car in front of the apartment and taking a cab at night when we went out. Then if Scotty came by, he'd think the boys were home.

The Right Touch

Some coaches get mad and just yell. Scotty knew how to handle the players individually to get the best out of everyone. Scotty might scream at a guy or pat him on the back. You never knew what to expect.

He'd walk in the dressing room before a game and say something like, "Big, tough, Noel Picard. You know what the word in the league is now? Noel Picard's a talker."

Noel would yell, "Who says that? I'll kill him!"

Scotty would say to us, "There, he's talking again."

Noel would say, "Hey, I'll kill anybody who says that!"

Scotty would shrug his shoulders and say, "See? Talking again."

Then he'd walk out of the room, and Noel would be going nuts. Noel was as big and as tough as they come, but you know what? Maybe Noel had been getting too fancy on the ice.

But that night, watch out! We were in Philadelphia, and Scotty tapped Noel and me to start the game. Noel jumped on the ice and banged and scrapped and hit.

The Philadelphia team probably said, "Who woke him up?"

The answer was, "Scotty. Who else?"

Red Alert

Scotty knew how to get you going if you were struggling. Even a guy like Red Berenson. Scotty wouldn't scream "you stink" at a veteran like Red. Here's how Scotty got to Red.

He'd say, "Red, it's my fault. I want to win so bad, and I know you want to win more than anyone else here, and I've got you playing too much.

"You're on the power play. You're killing penalties. You're playing a regular shift. Then I'm double-shifting you. You're on the ice at the end of every period.

"It's my fault. These other guys get a paycheck, too. Let them earn it. Because you're tired."

Red would yell, "I'm not tired!"

Scotty would say, "Yeah, you are, but it's my fault. I'll give you a rest. Don't play the power play."

Red would yell, "I want to play the power play."

Scotty would say, "You know what? Tomorrow, you won't even practice. Don't even come to practice. Just rest and stay home with the family."

Scotty did cut Red's ice time way back. Red didn't see the power play and he didn't double-shift. Scotty did keep him off the ice the next day.

And when Red finally did get out there, he was just flying.

Kennel Time

When it's time for a line change, the coach taps someone and says, "You're up next," or "Your line's next."

But there were times, if we weren't playing well, when Scotty wouldn't say anything. It would be time to change and somebody would say, "Scotty, who's up next?"

Scotty would have his chin in the air and he'd say, "Any five dogs!"

Or it might be, "Next five dogs!"

We were insulted by that, but that's what it was supposed to do.

The players pretty well knew who was up next. You have kind of a rotation going anyhow. So one of the older players like Red would send the lines out. If you scored a goal on one of those shifts, you'd come back to the bench and say, "Great line change, Red!" Not really loud...but Scotty heard everything.

The thing is, he wanted us to try to stick it to him. That was the whole point. And he'd never really compliment you.

Back then, Junior C was the lowest hockey, then Junior B and Junior A. If you made a bad pass with the puck at practice, Scotty would say, "Junior C!" A good pass, "Junior B!" A great pass, "Junior A!"

A really great pass was, "Awww, minor league!"

In Scotty's three years in St. Louis, I don't think we ever had an NHL pass.

Go Figure

Some players didn't like Scotty because they thought he was crazy. Even today, Noel Picard won't say too many good things about Scotty.

One night we went in to play in Montreal, then we went on to play at Toronto, then we had a day off before we played in Philadelphia. Noel is from Montreal, so that first night on the trip he had to get 17 tickets for his family. Scotty helped get them. Every game, you always had two extra players on the team who would go out for warmups and then not get to play.

At the time, we had this little gong in the dressing room, like the Gong Show. After warmups, Jean-Guy Talbot would take the gong and go over by the two guys we thought would be scratched. And he would gong each of them. We never knew for sure until somebody came in and left a ticket for the guys who were scratched. They needed tickets because they sat in the stands, not in the pressbox like the extra players do now.

This night in Montreal, Jean-Guy Talbot went around like he always did and gonged a couple of guys. Noel and myself never got gonged. We were defense partners and we always played. Then Scotty came in. He didn't say a word. He just walked around the room. When Scotty got to Noel and me, he put the two tickets on the bench between us. He did it real quick and got out of there fast. And it's a good thing he did.

Noel didn't even realize it when Scotty first put the tickets down. Then he started going crazy. He was kicking things in the bathroom. He wanted to kill Scotty.

Hey, Noel's family was all there and now he wasn't playing. And he had to pay for the 17 tickets. They weren't free.

I didn't understand it and I was mad, too. I didn't know what to say. But I thought, "There's a reason. I don't know if I was playing bad at the time, but there's a reason." That's the respect I had for Scotty.

We got beat bad and then we went to Toronto. And Jean-Guy wasn't gonging anybody before that game! We all sat in the dressing room wondering who would get gonged by Scotty this time. And you know who? Noel and myself. This time Scotty sent the trainer, Tommy Woodcock, to tell us.

Noel wouldn't talk to anybody, he was so mad. We were afraid he would try to go after Scotty. And Scotty probably thought the same thing, which is why he sent Tommy Woodcock in with the tickets.

We got beat bad again. We had a day off and then we went in to play Philadelphia. Scotty came in the dressing room before the game and went right where Noel and I were sitting. Noel wouldn't talk to Scotty, wouldn't even look at him.

Scotty said, "I just wanted to prove something. We have a scared hockey team without these two guys. We need these two guys to win, and you other guys proved that."

Now we're the best part of the team!

You look back and you see that the team had been going pretty bad when we got to Montreal. We never beat the Canadiens anyway. Toronto was a tough place to win, too.

In Philadelphia we started playing teams in our division, the other expansion teams. Those were games we had to win on the road.

So there was a reason that Scotty sat us out. That was his way of shaking up a team.

Noel still wanted to kill him, though.

You Are What You Eat

I always had a problem with weight.

One time, Scotty was sitting in the front of the bus when I got on. He said, "What are you eating?"

I said, "A chocolate bar."

He said, "Why?"

I said, "Energy."

They didn't have the energy bars then like they do now.

I went in the back and sat down. The bus took off. All of a sudden, Scotty came right back in front of me. He was talking to me, but everyone could hear.

He said, "Do you really believe in that?"

I said, "What?"

He said, "That chocolate gives you energy."

I said, "Yeah."

Scotty said, "Try eating fish. It's supposed to be a brain food."

The Answer Man

Dan Kelly, our broadcaster, would tell me: "Scotty's coming after you in the dressing room tonight. And he likes it when you give him that answer back, something stupid when he asks you a question."

Dan said Scotty would listen outside the dressing room door before a game. If it was too quiet, that meant the guys were nervous, too tight. Scotty knew he had to do something to get us ready to play. So he'd come into the dressing room and stand there, chin up, hand in the pockets, jingling the loose change.

He'd look around the room at each guy. All the way around the room. Twice. Nobody would say anything. I'd be in the corner, taping my stick. I'd look up and Scotty would be staring at me.

I'd say, "Okay, Scotty, what is it now?"

Scotty would say something like, "Look, look! He looks like he's seven months pregnant!"

I always had the little gut.

I'd say, "Scotty, the way you've been screwing me, it's a wonder I ain't!"

Then he'd charge out of the room and slam the door. The guys would say to me, "Why do you do that? He's going to trade you!"

But they were laughing. And Scotty'd be outside the door, listening.

And he'd know, "Now they're loose, now they're ready."

Key Player

The third year of the Blues, the 1969-1970 season, our owners the Salomons worked something out with a car dealer. Every player received a Barracuda to drive that season. The cars had a white bottom, blue top and the Bluenote on the door. All the same.

If we were going to Pat's Bar and Grill after practice, it'd be 20 cars there. Remember, we went everywhere as a team. We'd sign autographs and eat and do it all together.

One time, we were having a party at a place on Manchester Road, which is gone now. There was a Blues car there so I pulled in beside it. Somebody pulled next to me. Somebody else pulled next to him. And we filled up the lot. You never know your license plate number, of course, and all the cars looked alike.

Scotty was there that night. And the next day at practice, he said: "I don't like these cars. You guys are so stupid, each one of you has to go down the line with his key, trying to find which car is his."

Then Scotty said, "Oh, excuse me, fellas. I'm wrong. We've got one person who has no problem."

Everyone was waiting for the name.

Scotty said, "Bob Plager."

I was thinking, "Good! It's something good for a change from Scotty."

He said, "Bob Plager never has a problem finding his car. And the reason is, it's the only one left on the lot."

Mistaken Identity

One year, we're playing Boston in St. Louis. Pie McKenzie came in off the right wing and took a shot that hit off our crossbar behind Glenn Hall. But the red light came on for a goal being scored.

The Bruins were celebrating. The referee was Bob Sloan, and he didn't blow the whistle. So Al Arbour picked up the puck and skated down the ice. And Al, who scored zero to one goals per year, scored on Gerry Cheevers.

We started celebrating. Right now, it was a goal for St. Louis and no goal for Boston.

Then the Boston players attacked Sloan and started arguing. Harry Sinden, their coach, came part way onto the ice. The Bruins pinned the referee to the boards, yelling at him. And Sloan, on his way to the penalty box to tell the official scorer about our goal, changed his mind. He gave the goal to Boston.

So it's no goal for St. Louis. And now it's our turn to go after Sloan.

Our players were all around the penalty box, screaming at Sloan: "How can you change your mind?" And some other things we can't print here. Sloan had his face to the glass, still talking to the official scorer. Barc poked Sloan in the back with his stick. Al punched Sloan from behind in the shoulder.

Sloan turned around and I got in his face and argued. I received a penalty and got thrown out of the game.

One of a kind: Scotty Bowman's ear tug probably had some deep meaning that we were all too dumb to figure out. *(Bruce Bennett Studios)*

The next day the referee's report said that I speared Sloan in the back with my stick and punched him on the shoulder. So I had to go see the commissioner, Clarence Campbell.

I told Scotty it wasn't me. Channel 2, which is next door to The Arena, had film on the game. Scotty and I went over and watched the incident on film. It's very clear who did what.

I said, "See, Scotty? It was Barc who speared the referee and Al who punched him. We'll take that film and show it to Campbell."

Scotty's answer was: "We'll talk to Campbell, but we're not bringing the film."

I said, "What?"

Scotty said, "I'd sooner have you suspended than those two guys."

For the good of the team, he was probably right. As it turned out, I got fined but not suspended.

Merry Christmas

The first year of the Blues, we played on Christmas Day in Minnesota.

Usually you left the day before a road game. That was a league rule in case you had bad weather. This time, because it was Christmas, we left that same day.

We had a charter DC-3, which was a big deal. We never took charters back then. Everybody flew commercial. That was one of the firsts by the Salomons, our owners. They wanted us to open presents with our families on Christmas morning.

So, we chartered to Minnesota just in time for our pregame meal at the hotel, just across from the rink. We didn't even check in. Scotty had our pregame meeting right there in the room where we ate.

In the meeting, he had something to say about every player. And it wasn't good.

Scotty stood up and said, "Bob Plager, swinger…Jimmy Roberts, skates like he's got snow shoes on…Craig Cameron, should be playing in Hawaii—he goes to the corner like a hula dancer."

And Scotty had his hands and hips waving like he was doing the hula.

This is Christmas Day, remember. We all had our heads down, and little grins, but you don't dare say anything or let Scotty see you smiling. After the meeting, Scotty threw one key on the table and said, "That's your room."

For the whole team.

Nobody knew what to think. Scotty walked out and Red Berenson grabbed the key. We all went up to the room, Red opened the door, and it was twin beds.

Red jumped on one bed. A bunch of guys jumped on the other one. The rest of us stretched out on the floor. That was about 2 p.m. We didn't go over to the rink until about 5 p.m. So we all just tried to rest the best we could.

In the meeting, Scotty had also said, "Noel Picard, tonight, power play. You don't get on the ice any other time. But as soon as they get a penalty, you jump on the ice and you're right point.

"Bob Plager, if we take a penalty, don't you even look at me. You jump on the ice, penalty kill, left defense."

Noel and I were partners on defense. But Scotty said, "That's the only times you two guys see the ice. Power play, Noel Picard. Penalty kill, Bob Plager."

And the goalie who played that night, Seth Martin—he didn't play much.

The other thing about this is that December 25 is Christmas, but it's also Noel Picard's birthday.

Then the game started. When we had a power play, Noel jumped on the ice, right point. When we had a penalty to kill, I jumped on the ice, left defense. We went to the third period with no score. We were getting outplayed and outshot. Minnesota hit three goal posts and Seth Martin made some great saves, just unbelievable.

Noel and I looked at each other on the bench and we were smiling. We were hardly playing, so it wasn't our fault.

Scotty saw us. He came down and said, "You two think it's funny? Get out there, both of you!"

There was a stoppage and a faceoff in Minnesota's end, right-wing side. Noel was on the right point. We won the draw back to Noel. He shot, he scored and we won the game one to nothing.

That was Noel Picard's first goal in the NHL. The game winner. On Christmas Day. On his birthday.

After the game, the bus took us to the airport to our DC-3 charter, which was noisy and cold. We never drank on flights, ever, because we always flew commercial. And they had no alcohol on the charter for us.

Noel was smiling. He and his wife had just had a baby, and he had two baby bottles in his shaving kit. He took them out and they were full of his favorite drink. And it wasn't formula.

Noel was French and his English wasn't great. But he had his drinks. All of a sudden, it was, "Bobby, Bobby! What the score of the game?"

I said, "One to nothing, St. Louis Blues!"

Noel said, "Who score the goal?"

I said, "No-el Pee-card!"

Noel said, "Who he play with?"

I said, "Bob-bee Play-ger!"

We were at the back of the plane, but we were yelling loud enough for Scotty to hear up at the front.

And Scotty probably thought, "Just the way I planned it!"

Method and Madness

Nobody has ever figured Scotty out yet. To me, when he did those strange things, they were probably well-thought out. Whatever he did, worked. We didn't know why he put us all in the same room that Christmas Day, or why Noel and I hardly played.

But, we won the game.

Scotty just had something no other coach had. That's why he retired in 2002 in Detroit with nine Stanley Cups as a coach—the most ever—and why he won with three different teams.

One time, years after I quit playing, Scotty and I were talking. He said, "How'd the guys like Kansas City when they got sent down?"

Kansas City was the Blues' farm club then. Players who were hurt went down to get in shape before Scotty would put them in the Blues lineup again.

I said, "What do you mean?"

He laughed and said, "You didn't even know? You players never figured out what was going on?"

He said before he sent anyone down, he'd wait until Kansas City was on a long trip. A guy would get there in time to put his gear on the bus and go play like four games in six nights. When the bus got back to Kansas City, there would be a message to send the guy back to St. Louis.

Scotty told me, "When you send a player down, put him on the bus right away. Make him play four games in six nights and stay in the not great hotels they use in the minors, where the meal money's not as good.

"Bring him right back after that to the big-league team, and he'll tell all the players, 'I never want to go down there again!' The other players hear that, and they don't want to go down there, either."

Scotty said that if you sent guys down and they only played home games, the guys are in the nice hotel where they live all year. The Kansas City players know all the nice places to go. All the fans know the players, they're the heroes, they go out and have parties and a great time.

Then when they come back to St. Louis, they tell their teammates, "Boy, this Kansas City is a great place!"

We never knew that, but that was Scotty's thinking.

Jukebox Blues

When we played in Pittsburgh, Scotty would have the pregame meal at this restaurant owned by Elroy Face, who'd been a relief pitcher with the Pirates.

We finished eating and Scotty got up to hold the team meeting like usual. There was a jukebox in the corner of the room. Scotty walked over and looked at it, with his hands in his pockets, jingling his change the way he did.

We were all watching him. He took a coin out of his pocket, put it in the jukebox and punched some numbers. The record started to fall down to play.

Scotty stuck his chin back up in the air and said, "Okay, fellas. Here's our team meeting."

He walked out just as the record started playing: "We're going to Kansas City, Kansas City here we come!"

No Match for Scotty

We would be on the road. And after we got back a week later Scotty would say, "Huh, I'm surprised you guys can even play any more, being out at the Arena Bar in Pittsburgh, partying all night."

We'd go to play Philly a few days later. We'd come back to St. Louis and hear, "So, you were out in Philadelphia, making fools of yourselves."

Guys would say, "Why doesn't he just tell us he's got a detective on us?"

I said, "I can save him some money. I'll write a diary of every place we go, and he can just pay me half of what he's paying the detective."

We went to play in Oakland. We had our practice in the afternoon and then we were off. There was a place in San Francisco we liked to go to, and the only guys who went were Noel Picard, Al Arbour, Jean-Guy Talbot, Barclay Plager and me.

We got home a few days later and Scotty said, "You guys like that San Francisco, everybody running around at Sam's. Let's all get drunk there and run around."

The five of us looked at each other. We knew none of us would squeal. That's why we thought he had a detective.

Scotty did this all year. Finally, in the summer I ran into Dan Kelly. He said, "You know how stupid you guys are? Scotty just sits there and laughs."

Here's what happened. We had a little smoking room down by the dressing room at The Arena. About 70 percent of us smoked in those days.

Dan said, "Every bar you're in has matches with the name on it. You pick them up when you're in there and bring them back home. Then you light up with them in the smoking room, and when you leave Scotty goes in and checks the matchbooks."

After that, we all bought lighters.

The Real World

With Scotty, we always practiced around 10:30 or 11 a.m. at The Arena. One day it was on the board, "Practice tomorrow at 9 a.m."

Everybody knew how long it was from your own place to the rink. We were all used to driving 15 minutes, 20 minutes, maybe 25 minutes. We'd never been in rush hour traffic.

The next day, we were rushing to get on the ice by 9 a.m. A few were even late when practice started.

Scotty said nothing.

We skated for 15 minutes and then he blew the whistle. We gathered around and he yelled, "Off the ice! We have a meeting back here at 3:30 this afternoon."

Everybody went out for lunch and hung out. At 3:30 everybody was in the dressing room, waiting for Scotty.

It was 3:35…3:40…3:45…3:50…and then Scotty came down.

He said, "I decided to speak to everybody individually. Go home and I'll start calling your houses at 4:30. And you better be at your phone when I call."

We got up to leave. It was about 4 o'clock. Now we had to fight the rush hour traffic going home. There were no cell phones back then. We had to be in our homes to take Scotty's call. So we all rushed home, fighting the traffic. I was late. It was after 5 o'clock when I got in.

My phone rang and it was, "Hello, Bob?"

I said, "Yes, Scotty."

He said, "Just think how lucky you are. Did you fight that traffic coming to the rink in the morning? People do that five days a week, all their lives. Did you fight that traffic going home in the evening? People do that five days a week, all their lives. See how fortunate you are?"

And he hung up.

He didn't call everybody, just a couple of us. The next day we had practice at the regular time.

I came in and told the guys, "You wonder why Scotty does things? Here's the message this time: You're lucky to play hockey for a living."

Later on, my brother Barc was the assistant coach in St. Louis when Jacques Demers was the head coach. We would tell Jacques these Scotty stories, and Jacques would do some of the things Scotty did.

One of them was to make the guys come to practice in the morning rush hour. That was the year, 1986, when we came just one goal short of going back to the Stanley Cup finals. And that was the farthest we've gotten since Scotty left in 1970.

The Bowman Bottom Line

Scotty always had a reason. That's why I always liked him. He usually didn't do things to Red Berenson and Glenn Hall and Al Arbour and Dickie Moore and Doug Harvey. They were older. They had won championships. They knew how to act.

The rest of us were younger. When Scotty would do his crazy things, we just laughed and shook our heads. But we learned. And when I was coaching 20 years later in Peoria, I did a lot of "Scotty things." I did the trick with the matchbooks to find out where the players went out at night.

I could hardly wait to do that one. Then I pulled them aside and said, "This is how dumb you guys are. Why don't you all buy lighters?"

When we played for Scotty in St. Louis, a lot of guys hated him. Until June. That's when the league sent the checks with our playoff share for going to the finals. We got that all three years that Scotty was here. The salaries were so much smaller then, and that playoff check was a big bonus.

So every June, for that one day, the guys would say, "You know, maybe Scotty's not so bad after all!"

And every year, after we'd go to the finals, Scotty would talk to us—chat with us socially—for just one day.

Scotty would stick that chin out and say, "I'll talk to you at the parade!"

Hazing Days of Winter

Every hockey league had initiations back then for rookies. You shaved all their body hair. Well, you didn't shave their head. You might do part of one eyebrow, but you got everything else.

You usually waited till the guy's girlfriend was coming in for Christmas. You'd be at practice and you'd sing that old Gillette razor jingle:

> *"To look sharp, and to feel sharp too*
> *There's a razor that's made just for you!"*

The rookies would know that one of them was getting shaved that day. So they'd stay out on the ice for two hours until the veterans all went home. They might not get it that day, but we'd always get them.

In Philly this one time, we initiated Ray Fortin. That's who my brother Barc roomed with that first year. Not only did Ray Fortin get shaved that night, but later that year I got him back for a practical joke.

We were back to Philly for a game, but this time we were staying in Hershey, Pennsylvania. We had practice there the day before the game, and when I came into the dressing room the toes were cut out of my socks.

Guys did that to each other all the time as a practical joke. I knew Ray did it. He said he didn't, but he had that little grin on his face. We were always playing jokes on each other.

I went back in the bathroom and saw his teeth in a cup. Ray had false teeth, upper and lower plates. He was still on the ice, so I took his teeth back to the hotel, got a little box and mailed them back to The Arena in St. Louis.

We went out that night to eat, and Ray had no teeth. The next day, we had our pregame meal, and he couldn't eat properly.

Guys came up to me saying, "Okay, Bob, give him back his teeth."

I said, "What do you mean?"

I wouldn't admit it. Then Barc got me alone and said, "That's enough. Give him back his teeth."

I said, "Barc, I don't have them."

He said, "I know you did it."

I said, "Well, I mailed them back to St. Louis."

At the time, I thought it was funny. But to see Ray walking around like that on that road trip—we were gone for about five days—I thought maybe I went a little too far.

Years later, Ray came in to play one of the Oldtimers Games we had in St. Louis. I hadn't seen him since he quit playing and went back to Quebec Province.

He saw me first and yelled, "Bobby! My teeth…no more!"

He opened his mouth and started pushing on them. They wouldn't come out. They were screwed in or pegged in.

And Ray was laughing. So he got the last laugh on me there.

Unfortunate Fortin

There's one more story about Ray Fortin and Philadelphia from our first year.

We were playing the Flyers in the playoffs, the sixth game of the conference championships, and we were up three games to two. It was best of seven games. We were one win away from the Stanley Cup finals.

The sixth game was in St. Louis. We were up by a goal late in the game, and the Flyers pulled the goalie. They scored with the extra attacker and tied the game.

In the overtime, Philly came down and shot the puck in our end just to kill time for a line change.

They were changing players. Nobody was in our end. Glenn Hall, our goalie, came out to stop the puck. Ray Fortin put his stick down to deflect the puck away, and it hit the tip of his stick. The puck just changed direction by five or six inches, and it slid past Glenn Hall into the open net.

So we lost. In overtime. At home.

We'd been up three games to one at one point. Now we have to go back to Philly for Game 7 with their fans. And Philly was the number-one team in our conference, which had the six expansion teams.

In our dressing room after Game 6, everyone went up to Ray Fortin and gave him a little pat on the back. He was a rookie defenseman who had been up and down all year.

We felt bad to lose, but we also felt bad for Ray Fortin. And nobody felt worse than Ray. We went out for a few beers after that game, and Ray got up and disappeared. We were worried about him, especially if we didn't win that next game in Philly.

Legendary Entrance

Before Game 7 in Philadelphia, we were having our pregame meal at the hotel. It was very quiet in the room. I noticed that Scotty kept looking out the window.

Scotty always had his meeting after the pregame meal. We were almost done eating and nobody was saying anything. Everybody was down. And Scotty kept looking out the window.

All of a sudden, Scotty smiled…and in walked Doug Harvey. I knew Doug because we had roomed together for two years in the minors at Baltimore. But nobody knew Doug Harvey was coming to Philly for Game 7. He was a player-coach in Kansas City, our farm club, and he wasn't playing much because he was 43 years old.

When he was with Montreal he won the Norris Trophy for best defenseman seven times. Bobby Orr won eight in a row, but he was just starting the year we're talking about, '68.

Doug Harvey was my idol, the greatest defenseman who ever lived. Everybody knew who he was when he came into that room, but nobody knew why he was there.

Doug said, "Hi, everybody, what's going on? Is that a steak there? Bring me one here, not too rare."

He sat down and started cutting into his potato. Nobody said anything. We were all just watching him eat.

Then Scotty stood up. He looked around and said:

"I'm sure you all know Doug here. Doug will be playing tonight. He's here for experience. He's been through this many times with all the Cups he won in Montreal. He's going to help settle us down."

Scotty talked for a while, and then he said, "Doug, do you have anything to say?"

You've got to picture 18 or 20 guys staring at Doug Harvey. Nobody said anything. Doug stood up, and he was still chewing his steak. He swallowed, and the food didn't go all the way down. He took a drink of water, and he chewed a little more. He took another drink of water, and he gargled a little bit.

He put the glass down, and he looked around the room. It was still all quiet. And then he said:

"Fellas, a wet bird doesn't fly at night."

Then he sat back down, and he kept eating.

Nobody knew what to say. Even Scotty was taken off guard. Scotty just said, "The bus leaves for the rink at 4 o'clock."

To this day, nobody knows what Doug meant. When we get together for a reunion or an oldtimer's game, nobody can explain it.

But, when things get quiet, one of us will always say, "Hey, fellas…a wet bird never flies at night!"

Master at Work

We needed Doug Harvey because Noel Picard was out for that series with a broken hand. That's why Ray Fortin was playing when he tipped the puck into our net.

So for Game 7, I'm playing defense with Doug. And Doug, who hasn't played hardly at all that year, goes out and slows the game down the way he wants. Or he speeds it up. It's all in his head, the way he controls the game.

What a move by Scotty Bowman. He knew, "The fans will be going crazy there in Philly. Doug Harvey can take these fans out of the game just by the way he controls the puck."

Doug plays a regular shift, and now he's killing a penalty, and now he goes behind the net and shoots the puck down the ice, and he's whistling!

Our goaltender is Glenn Hall. He can hear the whistling behind the net when Doug has the puck. Doug shoots the puck down the ice and there's a stoppage.

Glenn comes over to the bench and yells at Scotty, "Tell that guy to quit whistling out there!"

Glenn was always so nervous, and Doug was always so calm.

So now we're up 2 to 1 with a minute-something to go in the game. I'm on the ice with Doug. The Flyers move the puck around, and they have a couple good chances, and Glenn makes a couple good saves.

We finally get the puck out over our blue line. They bring it back in offsides, so we get a stoppage of play. Now they pull their goalie. There's a little less than a minute left. Of course, we're thinking about the last game that we played, when they tied it up with the goalie pulled in the last minute and won it in overtime.

I'm out there and I'm tired. Doug and I have been out there for a while. I'm looking over at the bench, wondering if Scotty will make a line change.

Before he can send anybody out, Doug yells, "Don't worry Scotty, we're all right!"

I want to say, "Doug, speak for yourself!"

The faceoff is outside our blue line on the left side, where I am. Lou Angotti is Philly's best man on the draw, but Red Berenson is taking the faceoff for us. Red is on his forehand. He's going to whack it down the ice to keep it out of our zone, instead of pulling it back to our defense the way he normally would.

The defenders: Glenn Hall and Doug Harvey (2) protect our goal in the '68 finals from Montreal's Yvon Cournoyer (12) and Jacques Lemaire (25), now the coach in Minnesota. *(Bruce Bennett Studios)*

The official drops the puck. And as it hits the ice, in one motion Red goes forward with his stick and hits it. And it rolls all the way down into the empty net.

I was so happy that I stayed on the ice for the last few seconds. I wasn't tired any more.

And Doug Harvey was chosen one of the stars of the game.

Bad Influence...

I give Doug Harvey a big part of the credit for putting me in the NHL. I lived with him for two years in Baltimore earlier in the '60s when we both belonged to the Rangers.

Here I was, a kid, rooming with Doug the Legend. Ken Schinkel was in the apartment with us and there was always a fourth guy, who would change.

Doug was like a god to me. And he was crazy and fun. He had a big black Cadillac. We went to a restaurant one time, and Doug threw his keys to a guy in front of the restaurant and said, "Park this, please."

Doug loved wine, and he had a couple of glasses while we were eating. We came out, Doug looked around and said, "Where's the guy who parks the cars?"

We found a manager inside. He said, "We don't have a guy who parks cars."

It was just some guy standing there and he drove off with Doug's Cadillac. It turned up a day or two later by the mall near our apartment. It wasn't destroyed, it was just out of gas.

It didn't seem to bother Doug.

Back then I was very young, with a lot of learning to do. I saw that Doug had a good time. He drank—sometimes to much—but he never brought it to the rink. It didn't seem to interfere with how he played.

There's an old saying in hockey that Doug used: "Tomorrow we play guilty."

I tried to keep up with him off the ice, which was stupid and very tough. He had 20 years experience on me on the ice, and 20 years experience on me off the ice.

I don't drink now but I used that saying all the time when I played. I'd tell my brother Barc after I'd been out, "It's okay. I played some of my best games guilty."

Barc would say, "Maybe you did, but you can't play 70 of them like that!"

...*Good Influence*

In Baltimore, Doug and I didn't talk much hockey around the apartment or when we went out. I'd have liked that, but Doug didn't do that.

Meanwhile, the general manager of the Rangers, Emile Francis, called me and said he didn't have very good reports on how I was playing. There was a minor league team in Springfield, Massachusetts, and that was the worst place to go.

Eddie Shore was the coach, owner and general manager in Springfield, and he was so tough on the players there. That's how the players' union started, really, because of the hard way he treated his guys.

Emile said to me, "You've got one week to start playing better or we're sending you to Springfield."

I thought, "Oh, no."

So I said to Doug, "What am I doing wrong out there?"
And Doug said, "I thought you'd never ask."

That's why he didn't talk hockey with me away from the rink. He said, "I don't tell people how to play unless they come up to me with a question."

So we started talking hockey back at the apartment and everywhere else. He was just waiting for the kid to show interest.

Simple Wisdom

Doug would tell me, "The game is simple. So if you keep the game simple, you'll be all right."

The first thing I learned from him was, "If you don't have the puck, you can't make a mistake with it."

It's so simple, and it's so true.

He'd say, "If your partner's open, give him the puck and let him make the mistake. The longer you hold the puck, the longer the other team has to fill the lanes and pick off your pass. You're always thinking *before* you get the puck: If it's coming here, I'm going to put it there."

We had a 15-minute warmup before games then, and at the end we'd all line up and take turns shooting at our goalie. There was only one puck. If there were two pucks, Glenn Hall would get off the ice. He wasn't going to get hit any more than he had to.

I stood out there by the blue line, waiting with all the other guys to take a shot. Doug skated up and said, "When did you ever score from the blue line? With your shot, the puck might not even get there."

He told me to turn around and watch the other team in warmups. He always got the other team's lineup in the dressing room before the game, and he'd go through every player and his number. Then he would study each guy on the ice in the warmup.

Remember, in those days, there were no videos. Now, the players see everyone on tape as much as they want before a game. But back then, you had to play a team three or four times till you got to know what each player could do.

Doug and I would go out for a faceoff, and I'd be on left defense. Before they'd drop the puck Doug would say, "Who's the right winger?"

I'd start to look and Doug would say, "Don't look! Who is it? You should know that."

His point was it might be a big tough guy or it might be a speedy guy. When there's a line change, sometimes it happens fast and guys don't really pay attention.

Obviously, it's important to know whom you're playing against.

Listen and Learn

During the game, Doug had these little sayings that he used to teach you.

Sometimes you try to pass the puck through the players in the center of the ice because it looks open. I threw a cross-ice pass one time and it got intercepted. When I came back to the bench, Doug said, "Don't look now, but we have an extra player on the ice."

I said, "Where? Where?"

Doug said, "He's the best passer there is. And he shows up every shift of every game."

I said, "Who?"

And he said, "The boards. Learn to use the boards to pass the puck. Bank it around guys instead of trying to throw it through them."

Or, Doug would say, "The coach says no cross-ice passes, no drop passes, dump the puck in."

I'd say, "I didn't hear Scotty say that."

Doug would point up at the clock.

"That's the coach," he'd say. "The coach always tells you how to play. If there's two minutes left in the game and you're up a goal, the coach says, 'Play it safe. We don't need another goal.'

"If we're down a goal and you look up and see two or three minutes left, the coach says, 'Jump into the play, pinch in at their blueline, take chances. We need offense.'"

You hear things like that enough and they become automatic. Not just with me. With my players when I coached in the minors in Peoria.

We'd be up a goal late in the game, and you'd hear on the bench, "Boys, the best coach in hockey says dump it in."

I hadn't said anything. But they'd heard it from my Doug Harvey stories. And my Scotty Bowman stories. And they'll be using that stuff to teach when they quit playing and start to coach somewhere.

Red's Six Pack

Ed Van Impe played defense for Philadelphia, and he was a mean, tough hockey player. He was a stick man. If you went around him, he was known to crack the stick over your arm or across your ankles. You were going to pay the price. A lot of players slowed down or dumped the puck in when they got near him.

The Red Baron: When Red Berenson (7) was around, Noel (in back) and I tried to get him the puck and get out of his way. *(Bruce Bennett Studios)*

Red Berenson was our best player in those first years of the Blues. You always take care of your best player. You stick up for him. Red was our bread and butter.

We said, "Nobody bothers Red. You don't touch Red."

That was our job. Noel Picard and me especially, and Barc, too. But everybody's.

Van Impe would go after Red. And Noel would go after Van Impe if he touched Red or any of our players.

Van Impe wanted no part of Noel. He had to show up if Noel wanted to fight him, but he would hold his stick up to keep Noel away.

Before the '68-'69 season, we played an exhibition game at either Flint or Port Huron. We played Philly and Van Impe is out there. I didn't dress for that exhibition, but it was said in the dressing room, "Send a message to Van Impe to stay away from Red."

Barc ended up fighting Van Impe, and Barc got the best of the fight. Later on Noel got into it with Van Impe, and Noel beat him good.

When Van Impe went to the penalty box for fighting, I was in my civvies, sitting in the stands. I went over there and yelled, "Don't mess with Red!"

We were trying to get Red enough room to skate against Philly for the rest of the year. That was the message. We thought it was sent. And we found out it *was* sent. We found out on November 7, 1968, in Philadelphia—the night that Red scored his six goals.

If you listen to the record of Dan Kelly announcing that game, it's like: "Red Berenson goes down the ice…around Van Impe…goal!"

And then, "Red Berenson goes around Van Impe…goal!"

And then, "Red Berenson goes around Van Impe…goal!"

All six goals, Van Impe was on the ice. After about the fourth goal, he broke his stick on the back of Red's legs. After four goals, I guess I'd do that, too.

Only one other NHL player had scored six goals in one game. It was a great accomplishment for Red. But a lot of credit goes to the guys who got Red all that room, Noel and Barc and a lot of us who sent the message to Van Impe all season long.

We won the game 8-nothing. Scotty played Red a ton, trying to help him get the record. Jacques Plante was the goalie for us, and he had a little bonus in his contract for shutouts.

We had a stoppage once it was 8-nothing. Jacques skated over to the bench and said, "Fellas, we don't need any more goals. We've got a shutout going!"

Jacques ended up getting his bonus.

We came back to St. Louis, and the Salomons had a night for Red at The Arena. He got a brand new car from the Salomons and a canoe and a shotgun from the players.

You know what Van Impe got? Minus six. He was out there for every goal.

Say what you will about Philadelphia fans, how hard they are on visiting teams. When Red kept scoring, they started cheering. They gave him a standing ovation for the sixth goal. It was just as loud a cheer as he would have gotten at home. But that was the only time the Philadelphia fans ever cheered us.

And one of the next times we played there, I went up in the stands to visit some of them.

Up Close and Impersonal

We were playing in Philadelphia on January 6, 1972. We didn't think the refereeing was fair. We were down 2-nothing, and some of the calls led to the goals.

Scotty had gone to Montreal, and Al Arbour was our coach. Al got on the referee at the end of the second period and received a bench-minor penalty for arguing. They announced it as we were going to our dressing room.

The ramp was right behind our bench. There was no canopy over the ramp in those days, like they roll out there now to protect the players. Back then, you had to walk past with the fans hanging over you. They would throw things and they would yell. They were close enough that they could touch you and you could touch them.

When Al got the penalty, he was on the ice with the officials. They skated off to their dressing room at the other end of the rink, at the Zamboni entrance. Al followed them across the ice to keep arguing. I saw that, and I was an alternate captain then, so I followed him down.

Al caught the referee on the ramp at the Zamboni end. A fan came down and threw a beer on Al and took a swing at him. I was right behind Al, and a couple of our players were behind me. The rest were already in our dressing room.

I came off the ice and climbed up over the railing into the seats after the guy who threw the punch. The next thing you know, a bunch of fans were throwing things at Al and me. Then our players came up after me into the stands.

At the time, you thought it was the right thing to do. You're a little older now, and you think maybe it wasn't. But in the heat of the game you're protecting your coach.

It got very ugly. The police got involved, but they came after us instead of the fans who started it.

Al was busy down there on the ramp with the police. He had his shirt ripped off. He was only wearing a T-shirt and there was a lot of blood. Al got hit over the head. I think a policeman hit him with a night stick or a billy club. I don't know for sure, because I was busy.

I reached out and grabbed the fan who swung at Al. All the fans up there came in on me, but the team came in behind me. Phil Roberto was there, and my brother Barc, and my brother Billy. John Arbour—no relation to Al— was there. It was his first game up from the minors, and he got hit pretty good.

Family fun in Philly: That's me (5) and Barc (8) saying "Hi!" to the fan who attacked Al Arbour, with Billy (23) on the way after he escapes the guy in the white shirt. Anybody see my stick and gloves? *(Bruce Bennett Studios)*

Those were the first ones.

From what I understand, someone in our locker room said, "There's a fight in the stands!" And nobody had to say, "Let's go!" They just went to help us.

The riot squad was sent to the rink. The Philadelphia papers said more than 150 cops were brought in. They had started the game with just 17 policemen in uniform at the rink. The riot squad had bigger sticks than us, not the little "billies" that the regular cops had.

It went on for a *long* time. When it finally broke up, we skated back to our bench to go to the dressing room. Fans were reaching over the boards, spitting, kicking at us, throwing things at us.

Floyd Thomson, on his way off the ice, had his stick up in the air for protection. A policeman in the runway grabbed his stick. Floyd pulled it back. The policeman tried to pull it out of his hands. Floyd wouldn't let go. The policeman kept pulling. Finally, Floyd let go…and the stick hit the policeman in the head and knocked his hat off.

The game was going to be called off. There was a big discussion. They wanted to take the ones to jail who went up in the stands. But Al said, "Nobody's going to jail because we have a game to finish."

The police decided to let us play the third period, but the game was delayed a long time, 35 or 45 minutes. And not just because of the brawl. We all had to have our skates sharpened during the intermission. We had nicks in the blades from going up in the stands. They had to be ground down pretty far, because the nicks were in there pretty good.

Tommy Woodcock, our trainer, was busy. He was sharpening skates *and* putting stitches in.

John Arbour and Al Arbour had their heads cut open. Al just got 12 stitches, but they put them in big in those days!

Crime and
Semi-punishment

When we came out for the third period, the police were in the runway outside our door with a list of the players to be arrested.

I'm always the last guy off the ice at the end of a period, and I'm always the last guy out of the dressing room to start a period. That started when I was just called up from juniors to the minors in Baltimore. We were in Springfield, and at the end of the period I was one of the first guys off the ice. I was in the dressing room by the time someone said, "There's a fight out on the runway!" When I got there, it was about over. Some fans had attacked one of our players, and I didn't have a chance to get involved.

So ever since then, I made sure all the players got off the ice first and got on the ice first. Then I followed, so if anything happened, I'd be there to help and protect. That's why in this thing with Al in Philly, I was the last guy waiting to get off the ice. I saw he was arguing, and when he went off the bench, I went with him.

To help and protect. That's all. Just like the cops!

So I was the first in the stands. And the Philly papers said the next day that I instigated it all—not the fan who threw the drink and the swing at Al.

Anyway, we opened the door to the locker room to go out for the third period. The runway to the bench was lined with policemen—the riot squad with their big night sticks. A police captain was there with a list. The other policemen were pointing out names and numbers of who was in the fight.

Al Arbour, John Arbour, Floyd Thomson, and Phil Roberto all went out and all had their names written down. I was at the end of the line. When I saw all this I hid back in the dressing room. After the players had all left, I told Tommy Woodcock, "The cops are taking names. Go out and lock the door. When they're all gone, come back and get me."

So Tommy went out and locked the door, with me listening on the other side. The policeman said, "Is that it?" Tommy said, "That's it."

He went down to the bench. The third period started. The cops went away. Tommy came back to let me out. I sneaked down, sat at the end of the bench and took my regular shift.

Al was standing there coaching in his T-shirt and suit coat. Dan Kelly, our broadcaster, said he looked like Art Carney from *The Honeymooners*.

All period, the fans went crazy, yelling and screaming. We were down 2-nothing but we were all pumped up. We had just done something as a team. We stood up for our coach and each other.

And I think the Philadelphia players, sitting in the dressing room all that time, got a little bit cold. We had to kill that two-minute penalty to Al that started the whole brawl. And we did kill it. Shortly after that, we got two goals from Garry Unger and Phil Roberto, two of the guys who came into the stands after me, to tie it up.

Gary Sabourin scored later and we won, 3-2.

Jail On!

That was just the game. Then there was jail.

As we came off the ice to the dressing room, the police captain was there with some policemen. As the team came by, they checked the sweater numbers and the names on the sheet.

Al Arbour. John Arbour. Floyd Thomson. Phil Roberto.

The cops went into the dressing room and waited till the guys showered and changed. Then they escorted the players and Al to the paddy wagon. I was watching and waiting, but nobody was waiting for me. There was no No. 5 on the list.

Our guys were charged with instigating a riot, except for Floyd. He was charged with assaulting an officer when he let the stick go when the cop pulled on it.

Sid Salomon Jr. was on the trip, and he went with the guys to the police station. That's why he was such a great owner. The guys were kept till early in the morning. Then they were finally released on like $500 bond each.

Mr. Salomon blasted the police. He told the Philly papers it was "the worst case of police brutality since the 1968 Democratic convention in Chicago."

I felt sorry for the guys who got hauled off to jail. When the cops were taking them to the paddy wagon, I told the guys, "When you get out, I'll have some adult beverages waiting for you, all cooled down back at the hotel."

I got some beverages and filled my bathtub with ice for the guys who would be a little late. As it turned out, we had an early flight in the morning and the players in jail never made it back to the hotel.

So, I guess the cleaning lady probably had a little party after we checked out.

NHL Justice

I got out of going to jail in Philadelphia. But I still had to go to a hearing with Clarence Campbell, the NHL commissioner, in the league office in Montreal.

The referee and the linesmen had to make a report to the league office. And they all mentioned that I was the first one in the stands.

I was there with Al Arbour, Phil Roberto, John Arbour, Garry Unger and my brother Barc. Jim Cullen, the Blues lawyer, was with us. Floyd Thomson didn't have to go, because the referee and linesmen weren't there when his stick hit the cop.

I knew Mr. Campbell pretty well. They used to say I was on his carpet more than his vacuum cleaner. I always thought he was hard but he was fair.

He started to read the referee's report: "Bob Plager was the first one in the stands, he kept his gloves on, and he went up there swinging his stick."

I started to tell Mr. Campbell that I had dropped my stick and my gloves when I went into the crowd.

And I was told, "You'll get your chance to speak, and you can have as much time as you want then to state your case. But until then you don't say a thing."

So then they get the linesmen's written reports. The first linesman wrote: "I observed Bob Plager going into the stands with his gloves on, swinging his stick."

I still couldn't say anything.

The second linesman's report said: "I observed Bob Plager leaving the ice, swinging his stick, with his gloves still on."

Here's what saved me. They had two films from the game from different angles that showed us going into the stands. The officials wrote their reports before they knew about the films.

So then it was my turn. Being a little smart there, knowing I was right, I said, "Mr. Campbell, when the referee and the linesmen make a report, do they talk to each other first? Or do they each make a report on what they see themselves?"

Mr. Campbell said, "They don't get together and come up with one thing."

I was very excited when I heard that. I said I wanted to see the first film. They got a little projector and a screen, and I had a pointer. I said I'd like to answer the referee's report first.

We ran the film and I said, "As you know, I'm No. 5. There's Al Arbour going off the ice. Can we stop the film now? There I am, No. 5. Now run it a little more...There, stop it!

"Before I get off the ice, my gloves and stick are gone. Okay, run it a little more...Now here I am in the stands...No gloves, no stick...Now I'd like to get the other film out."

Jim Cullen said, "Bob..."

He thought I was going overboard. But I wanted to use my time. So they ran the second film, and I went through it again.

Then I said, "I think the referee made a mistake. But that happens. Now I'd like to do the first linesman."

So we ran both films again. I said, "So maybe the first linesman made a mistake. And that can happen. Let's rewind the film."

Mr. Campbell said, "Mr. Plager, we see your point."

And me, being a little smart, said, "Mr. Campbell, you told me I could take as much time as I wanted."

So we showed both films a third time to show that the other linesman was wrong.

Then I said, "Mr. Campbell, I think we have a problem. If they each make an individual report, and each one is wrong, I'm not saying they talked to each other, but there's something the matter."

I know I really peeved them all off, the way I was going on. Jim Cullen was nudging me, so I quit talking.

The other guys didn't have much to say. When we left, we each had to put up $1,000 bond until Mr. Campbell decided the punishment.

The reason we weren't fined right away, and this is why I respect Mr. Campbell, is that some fans had filed lawsuits in Philadelphia over this thing. He didn't want to declare us guilty of anything until the court cases were settled, or his ruling could hurt us in court.

I knew I was in trouble for being the first one up in the stands. But when the fines came down, I had one of the lesser amounts, about 250 bucks. Again, that's why Mr. Campbell was so fair: He knew I didn't do what the on-ice officials said I did.

I don't know what Mr. Campbell did with the linesmen and referee, but it looked like he was more peeved at them than he was at me.

Making Friends in Pittsburgh

In those days, the late '60s and early '70s, we had rivalries with every team. Pittsburgh was one of the biggest rivals. The Penguins had guys like Glen Sather, Bugsy Watson, and the Hextalls, Dennis and Bryan. These were guys who came to play every night, tough and scrappy.

So we had great games with them. We had many bench-clearing brawls. And the fans in Pittsburgh were really involved.

They had the "Bar-clay" chant going for my brother. They hung banners all around the rink. I remember one of them was: "Noel Picard Is Here Courtesy of the St. Louis Zoo." Another was: "Bucket Mouth Bowman and His Three Stooges: Barclay, Bob and Noel." I liked that one, but I'm not sure Scotty appreciated it.

We were in Pittsburgh one night, and Al Smith was their goaltender. In one of our brawls earlier that year, somebody was holding Barc down, and Al Smith came out of the net and sucker-punched him.

It was just a matter of time before Al Smith would get it. And it happened this night when the game was televised back in St. Louis. People back here still talk about it.

Things started when Noel Picard fought Dunc McCallum. While the officials broke that up, I went to the other end and told Smith, "No referee, no linesmen, let's go!"

He said, "No problem!"

He was more than willing. He was a scrapper, not your typical goalie. So we went at it. We exchanged punches, and we landed punches, and finally we got a little tired.

We weren't finished, but the linesmen came in and separated us.

Smith said, "I'll be back."

He skated over to his bench. He took off his sweater, his shoulder pads and his belly pad, put his braces back up and skated back to center ice.

I was there waiting for Round Two. And that one went good, too. We held each other with one hand and exchanged punches with the other hand. I threw a right. He threw a right. I'd duck it or get hit on top of the head, and so would he. Then I took my left hand, let go of his sweater and came up with the left. And that uppercut ended the fight. Someone said it broke his jaw.

So he was out of the game. And I was out of the game, because I got thrown out.

Now, when we skated in warmups in Pittsburgh, there was one section of the rink near our bench where the fans would yell and scream and hold the signs up. Barc would skate by in warmups and throw them a little kiss, to get them going even more.

When I got thrown out for fighting Smith, I went into the dressing room and showered and dressed. Then I went back out the ramp to watch the game. I turned toward that section where the fans really got on us, and a few rows from the ice there were four empty seats.

There was always a policeman there by our dressing room door. They did that just about everywhere, just like they had one in the penalty box for the visiting team. The policeman by our dressing room in Pittsburgh was there every game. He was a good guy…much better than the Philly cops!

I said, "Let's go for a walk."

He said, "Bob, what are you up to?"

I said, "Don't worry. Just come on."

We walked around to that one section and I started walking down the aisle. As I walked by each row, I heard people whispering, "Plager…that's Plager…hey, it's Plager!" I'd glance back, and the people I passed were all staring at me. Nobody knew what to say, and the people down below didn't know I was on my way.

I came to the row with the empty seats, which were in the middle of the row. I started in, saying really loud, "Excuse me, excuse me!" By then the people were all looking. I sat right down, and nobody knew what to say or what to do. I just watched the game like nothing was going on. It was real quiet.

Then, I turned to the people next to me and said, real loud, "Did that Plager kick the crap out of that Smith or what?"

They said, "He did not!"

I said, "Yes he did!"

They said, "He did not!"

But they had grins on their faces. Hey, I don't care how noisy other fans are. When you meet them somewhere, they always say, "Boy, I really hated you, but I respected you."

Then you've got a conversation going on. That's what happened in that section in Pittsburgh, where they hated us so bad.

Finally I said, "By the way, where's a good spot to go for a drink and a meal afterward?"

They all hung out at the same spot, Primanti Brothers, a great bar and restaurant. You get a burger there, and they put the fries on it and everything. It's like a five-course meal between two pieces of bread.

So after the game, I went—by myself—and put a few hours in with these people down at Primanti's. And it was great. They talked hockey. They loved the players.

Whenever we went back for a game, they still booed us and yelled and screamed and chanted "Bar-clay" at my brother.

In warmups, I'd skate around and they'd boo me, and I'd give them a mean look. And we'd all laugh. Then I'd get serious for the game and they'd start screaming at me again.

When I retired and started scouting, I would go to Pittsburgh to watch a game, and Primanti's was the place I'd go afterward. I'd go back behind the bar and serve drinks. I was a fixture there.

And whenever I go back now, I still am.

Blues Fans

St. Louis has the best fans in the NHL.

The Salomons had a lot to do with it when they started the Blues from scratch in '67. The way the Salomons treated people here, the players and the fans, was something special.

When they took over that old Arena it was so clean. The bathrooms were spotless. They had a full-time painter going around every day. That's all he did, touch up the paint in the building. Sid Salomon Jr., old Mr. Salomon, had an office in there, and every day he'd go around and walk the building and inspect.

The Arena was the place to be seen. Everything was first class. The games were a dress-up thing. I know people who bought new clothes to go to the games.

Down behind the Blues bench, where the Salomons sat, it was like a social club. The Salomons were one of the first owners to put in a place for people to eat and watch the game. They had the Arena Club, which anybody got into, and they had the Goaltenders Club, which was a membership club.

When we came on the ice to start the game the fans used to sing "When the Blues Come Marching In," to the tune of "When the Saints Come Marching In." The whole building would stand up and sing:

"We want to be among their number,
When the Blues come marching in."

It pumped you up. They were selling out that big building, and fans really thought it was *their* team. Fans would see you out in town, and they'd say, "*We* played great last night," or "*We* had a tough game."

You got to know the season ticket holders, where a lot of them sat. One time, I saw this woman in town and I said, "Were you sick last night?"

And she said, "How did you know that?"

I said, "You weren't at the game."

She said, "How did you know that?"

I said, "You sit five rows behind the penalty box. Hey, we stand for the national anthem, we look around and we see everybody."

Barc and I came down here that first year, and we had no family here. Our booster club was really big. We would spend time with the fans at their meetings, and they would say, "Do you want a home-cooked meal?"

So we went to people's houses for dinner. One family, Shirley and Bill Withrow, had us over many times. We went to their kids' birthday parties.

There are fans still going to the games that we've known since Day 1 in '67.

We were one big family, the players and the fans.

A Player's Owner

When the expansion came in, most players wanted to come to St. Louis to play for the Blues—because of the Salomons. They were the best owners in hockey.

In the old days, a dressing room was just a room where you hung your clothes. There was an old stickroom next door. And that was it. Mr. Salomon carpeted a new dressing room for us. He had two big whirlpool tubs in there and a big sauna. You used to hang your clothes up in the dressing room in your locker, with all your sweaty gear. He put in a changing room for your civilian clothes. He made it into a little lounge, with a TV set and a couch. And he put a pool table in a big room down the hall so the players could relax.

Nobody had anything like that anywhere else in the NHL.

After the game the wives used to stand and wait in the hall for the players, with the kids running around. So Mr. Salomon had a Wives Room built, with food in there. And the players could go in after the game with their families.

Nobody else had that, either.

Mr. Salomon said, "The Arena is where the players spend their time. It's their home away from home. Let's make it comfortable so they want to be here."

I couldn't forget the big Christmas cards the Salomons used to send us. Mr. Salomon would come down to the dressing room after a big win, and he'd pass out cigars to the players.

One time at practice, he was talking about this new TV set from Japan. I don't remember the details, but it had all this stuff that was new. And he said, "There are only about a hundred of them that came over to America so far. But I got 30 of them, and there will be one delivered to each of your houses today."

That TV lasted for a long time, too. I might even still have it in the basement somewhere. I don't throw much away!

But the big thing was after every season, the Salomons had the players and their families down to Florida for a week. The married guys took their kids out of school.

Mr. Salomon owned the Golden Strand, a hotel in Miami. Your room there was free and your food was free. They arranged for about 10 cars from a dealership for the players to use.

The Salomons always had one big night for the team, like at a Polynesian restaurant where they had a show. And they arranged for babysitters for the kids. And they'd have a big party for us at the penthouse where the Salomons stayed in the hotel.

Disney World had just opened up, and Mr. Salomon got buses and took the families up there.

After the vacation week was over, and the family guys went back and put their kids back in school, Mr. Salomon told the single guys, "Fellas, you can stay here as long as you want. You have to buy your own food and no cars, but the room is free."

When I was single, I used to spend a month down there. It was like a summer home.

The other owners in the league weren't too happy about all of that. Mr. Salomon was treating the players too well. That's why all the players wanted to play here.

And the players didn't want to disappoint these people—the Salomons and the fans. We didn't cheat anybody. Every player was like that. You didn't have good shifts every time. Some games weren't very good at all.

But we tried. And the Salomons and the fans recognized that.

Classy owners: Everybody in the NHL wanted to play for the Blues because of Sid Salomon Jr. (right) and Sid the "Two Plus One." *(Bruce Bennett Studios)*

Put 'em Up

People say, "Why were there so many fights back then?" Well, when I first came up to the NHL with the Rangers, there were six teams. You played every team 12 times a year, and you played them on back-to-back days. When we expanded to 12 teams, you still played the teams in your conference 10 times. If somebody did something to you, you were still mad when you saw them again. That's why we had rivalries.

Maybe you scrapped with a guy in juniors and then you scrapped with him again in the minors. It was different then before they had the Entry Draft for juniors. The junior teams were all affiliated with an NHL team, and you belonged to that NHL team. The same thing in the minors. You came through the system with the same guys and you played against the same guys. Until somebody got traded.

So you learned to hate players before you got to the NHL.

Now, Peterborough will have four guys get drafted by different NHL teams, so they're all buddy-buddy when they get to the NHL. We didn't have a chance to be buddy-buddy. You were in the NHL, but you still had feelings against these guys from when you were in the minors or juniors.

Might is Right

The guys weren't all goons back then. They were good hockey players.

Yeah, there were a lot of fights, but you picked your spots. And you didn't hurt the hockey team when you fought.

People would get traded to St. Louis, and you'd ask them, "What did you talk about in the dressing room when you came into St. Louis to play us?"

The first thing they would say is, "Don't watch your shots. Don't watch your passes. Watch out for the Plagers. Keep your head up. They'll throw that hip check and you'll get hit."

That's what a good body check does.

Plus, the other thing they'd say was that we had a pretty tough team. The fans never left the rink till the end of the game, no matter what the score was. Because the players held grudges.

You didn't want to do anything in the middle of the game or if the score was still close. You didn't want to take a penalty and put the other team on the power play and give them a goal.

If somebody gave you a cheap shot, and the score was 2-1 or 3-2, you'd say, "The time will come, the time will come." But if we were losing 4-1, with two or three minutes left in the game, you'd look down the bench. Noel Picard would say, "Bobby, you think we can still win this game?"

I'd say, "No way."

Noel would say, "Good! We punish now."

If you had it in for somebody, that's when you got even.

Noel would say, "Bobby, when do we play this team again?"

I'd say, "Next week."

Noel would say, "Good! We show them they shouldn't do this to us."

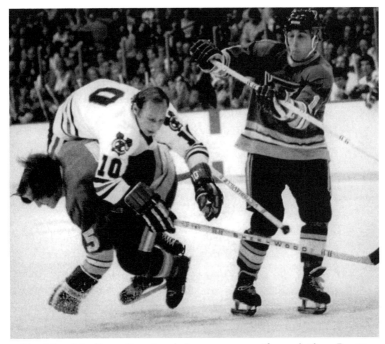

I'm hip: My favorite check bounces another victim, Brett Hull's uncle Dennis. *Doug Palazzari is at right. (Bruce Bennett Studios)*

A Knee for a Knee

So you had the rivalries going and you didn't like certain guys. But the day they got traded to your team, you were friends.

My second year in St. Louis, I got my knee operated on because of Derek Sanderson. We were playing the Bruins and it was near the end of the game. The whistle blew, the play was over and I relaxed. Derek stuck his knee out and he got me. And it was bad.

It was a dirty hit and he got away with it. There was not even a penalty.

I got up and skated back to the bench. There was pain, but nothing on my face. I didn't want him to know he hurt me.

When the game was over I got on the trainer's table, and they said the ligaments were torn right off the kneecap. They wanted to operate that night, but they waited till the next day, which was Thanksgiving.

After the game I was on crutches, and I was going out to my car. The bus with the Bruins drove by. Bad timing.

A window opened, and Derek Sanderson yelled out, "How's the knee, Bob?"

That's what hurt most, that he knew he hurt me. I yelled back, "Your time will come!"

I had put a lot of players out of the game with hits, and a lot had been operated on. But I never felt bad because they were clean hits. That was part of the game.

This was different.

I came back late in the season. The first time we played Boston, every time I skated past Sanderson I said, "I owe you…I'm going to get you…I owe you."

It was the first game, so he expected to get hit. Everybody expected him to get hit. But when I got him, it was going to be at the right time, and it was going to be a bad one.

I knew he was watching me that night. It really affected his play. He was doing things like slowing down when he went into the corner with me.

So I didn't do anything to him the first few times we played. I'd skate past him and say, "It could be tonight, but it won't be pretty." I always thought I owned him, because he'd be watching me. His mind was on me. I was in no hurry, but I was going to get him.

Then one game I hit Derek with a hip check. He went up and over me. He got his knee hurt, and he got operated on.

When he finally came back, he was smiling. He said, "I guess we're even now."

I said, "Derek, my hit was clean. Yours was dirty. I'm still going to get you. And you'll know it. And it won't be pretty."

This went on for some years, even after he got traded to the Rangers. Then we were playing New York, and he jumped Claude Larose and fought him. We collided by our bench, and I grabbed Derek. I held him and I said, "It could be now."

He said, "You've been saying that for years. I don't think you have the guts."

I just said, "Well…" And I punched him in the face.

I proceeded to pound him pretty good. Nobody came to help him. Usually when a guy's getting beat up, somebody's going to jump in. You don't want to see a teammate get beat like that.

He took a lot of punches, and he had enough left to skate off the ice and hold his hands up like he'd won.

The next season, 1975-76, Derek Sanderson was traded to St. Louis. He came to the dressing room and he was a little shy.

I shook his hand and said, "What happened to you with New York will never happen here."

He lived out in my area. I didn't hang out with him, but we went out together when it was a team function. You hold a grudge, but when you're a teammate, you say, "I'll stick up for you. I'll fight for you."

But when the guy gets traded away, then you hate him again.

The Record-setter

The first Blues game ever was against Minnesota on October 11, 1967. The game was a 2-2 tie.

On one of my first shifts I went out and whacked a guy with my stick. I whacked him pretty good and got sent to the penalty box for two minutes.

After the period, we were in the dressing room and guys said to me, "What did that guy do? He must have done something bad for you to whack him like that."

I said, "No, you don't understand. Every year the teams come out with their media guides. They have all the team records in there.

"This is the first game in the history of the St. Louis Blues. So as long as the Blues are here, when that book comes out every year I'll have my name in there—first penalty.

"That's one record nobody can ever break."

If you look in the Blues' media guide, I'm still in there.

First penalty: Bob Plager, October 11, 1967 (1:04 of first period).

As it turned out, I got in the book anyhow. I got the first assist in Blues history when Larry Keenan scored our first goal at 3:22 of the first period.

I didn't get many points. I only had 120 more assists in 11 years in St. Louis—and only 20 goals. So I wasn't taking any chances on getting into the record book on skill. That's why I took that first penalty.

A Medical First

J.G. Probstein was our team doctor that first season. He was 60 or 70 years old then, and he was great.

In our first game, Noel Picard got cut in the forehead and went off the ice for stitches. These were the first stitches for the St. Louis Blues, and the first time Doc Probstein put stitches in a hockey player during a game.

He was getting ready to start and Noel said, "Doctor, what are you doing?"

He said, "I'm going to freeze it so you don't feel anything when the stitches go in."

Noel said, "Doctor, they never freeze it. Just put the stitches in. I've got a hockey game to go to."

When Doc Probstein would tell the story, he always said, "So I sew Noel up and turn to get a bandage, and he's gone. I'm standing there, and a few seconds later Noel sticks his head around the corner and says, 'Doc, will you be here for a while?'

"I say yeah. And Noel says, 'Good! Because the guy who did this to me will be coming in soon.'"

What a Guy

Jean-Guy Talbot was the guy who ended Scotty Bowman's playing career. He hit Scotty over the head with a stick in junior hockey. I think Scotty had steel plates in his head from that, which may explain why Scotty thought so different from everyone else. But, anyway, the doctors said he couldn't play any more.

They both came up through the Montreal organization, Jean-Guy as a player and Scotty as a coach in juniors and the minors.

Our first season in St. Louis, Scotty had taken over as head coach. Jean-Guy was with Detroit and his name came up on waivers on January 13.

There was never any talk from Scotty that this is the guy who ended his career. If somebody could help the Blues, which Jean-Guy could and did, Scotty wanted him. Scotty looked at it as another ex-Montreal player who won a bunch of Stanley Cups—and a forward who played defense, too. We already had Jimmy Roberts as a forward-defenseman. You didn't dress as many players then, and Scotty liked guys who could play both positions.

As I said, those Montreal guys didn't just know how to win. You didn't turn your back on them. There was always something happening.

When you taped your stick, the tape would be too sticky. So we'd fill socks halfway up with foot powder or talcum powder, hit the sock against the stick, and the powder would take the stickiness off. One of those socks of powder was always near Jean-Guy in the locker room. Somebody in a dark suit and dark pants would be going out the door, and all of a sudden the sock would come flying across the room.

The powder would be all over the back of the suit. And Jean-Guy would just be sitting there, smiling.

Somebody would get out of the shower and pick up the hair dryer and turn it on. It would be filled with powder, too. The player would be covered and have to shower again. That never happened to me—I had short hair—but you knew where the powder came from.

Jean-Guy brought one big prank over from Montreal and taught me. The first person I tried it on was Noel Picard.

We were at practice on the road. Noel was still on the ice when I came into the locker room. He got all his clothes from this tailor back in Montreal, and he'd always talk about how great this tailor was.

So I'd grab Noel's pants, and I'd have a razor blade or the trainer's scalpel. I'd start with the seam below the belt loop in the back and cut every fourth or fifth stitch, all the way down and around to the fly.

Noel would put the pants on and not notice anything wrong. Usually after the game, when the team went out together, we'd be out walking. He'd get outside and nothing would happen right way. Then he'd take a big step or start up a stairway, and his pants would rip from the fly to the top of his belt in back. The seat would just come out of his pants.

I'd try to be close to him when it happened. The guys would say, "Geez, Noel, you need a new tailor."

For a while it was only Noel's pants we were getting, because we could always blame his tailor. Then I did it to some of my players when I coached in Peoria. And I also did it in the Blues dressing room the past few years. I was a pro scout then, and I'd always be away on the road when the stitches came apart.

That way they didn't suspect me. But I don't want to say which players. They're still here and could get me back!

Another Cut of Cloth

When Sid Salomon Jr. was here as our first owner, we always wore coats and ties when we traveled. As a hockey team, you were always taught to dress up because you represented the Blues and the City of St. Louis.

But just about every road trip back then, something would happen on the airplanes.

You never wanted to fall asleep on the plane—for a few reasons.

The trainers were allowed to carry scissors in their medical kits then. Now with the security against terrorism, they're not allowed to do that. But back then guys would be in their seats and see somebody get up—Jean-Guy, Noel, myself—to talk to the trainer. And the guys would smile and think, "Uh-oh, somebody's asleep."

That's when the scissors came out and a guy's tie was cut in half. You'd take the bottom part and the guy wouldn't notice it right away. He'd be walking around the airport, looking nice, with half a tie.

Mr. Salomon's son, Sid the third, was in his 30s back then. He was on a trip when he fell asleep on the plane.

And I got the dare: "Young Sid is asleep up in the front, Bob. You don't have the guts to cut his tie!"

So I got the scissors and did it. Everyone was grinning and laughing, but Young Sid never noticed. We got off the plane and went through the terminal and were waiting to get our bags before he caught on.

Young Sid was a great person. He smiled, and then he saw me. He had that look on his face and he was shaking his head.

He got his bag and walked by and said, "Okay, Bob." And of course I said, "Not me, not me!"

Payback

A while later back in St. Louis, I went down to the dressing room after one of our games, which we won. I put down my hockey equipment, looked up at my street clothes...and one leg was cut out of my pants.

I said nothing. I took my shower, taking my time, and I came back to my locker. I could see Young Sid and a couple of players around the corner, watching and wondering what would happen.

They didn't notice that I'd already noticed it.

I took my pants like nothing was the matter. I put on the leg that was cut. I put on the other leg. I put my shirt on. I tied my tie. I went over to the mirror and combed my hair. I came back and put on my coat and walked past them.

And I never said a word.

I walked back to the Wives Room with the rest of the players and their families. They were all laughing. I went on having something to eat, something to drink, and then I got up.

I still hadn't said a word. I went back to the dressing room, put on a pair of sweat pants with my coat and tie and went back out for the rest of the evening.

Payback II

L ater on that week, Mr. Salomon had a party over at his house for the players and wives. It was the first time we'd been to his house, and it was beautiful.

Barclay and I drove to the party. I got out of the car and rang the doorbell, standing there with the same pants that Sid the Third had cut the leg off.

One of the help answered the door. He didn't know whether he should let me in or not. Barc just shook his head. Barc shook his head a lot with me around.

Inside I again walked around like nothing happened. Sid the third saw me and came over, laughing and shaking his head.

I told him, "Sid, I'd like to apologize for looking this way. But I only have two pairs of pants, and the other one is in the cleaner's."

I wore those one-legged pants all night. I didn't bring anything to change into.

Later on, Young Sid came up to me with a check for $100, which was a lot of money then. He said, "Bobby, I'm sorry about your pants. Please take this."

I said, "Sid, I can't accept this. Your tie was probably worth twice as much as my pants!"

Airplane Antics

In our day, we traveled on commercial flights.

You had your little carry-on bags with the shaving kits. Every once in a while, you'd see the guys stand up and get their shaving kits out, or bend over if the bag was under their seat.

And that was the signal.

On long flights, to be comfortable you took your shoes off and put them under your seat. And the shoes would get passed up to the front. Somebody up there would have the shaving cream from his bag out and fill up just the toes, so you couldn't see the white stuff down in there.

Then the shoes would be passed back and put under the seat they came from. When the plane was ready to land, the player would put the first shoe on. The shaving cream would ooze out right when the guy was trying to get off the plane.

Or if a guy was sleeping, you might put shaving cream on the top of his head. Just pile it up there carefully so he wouldn't feel it. A lot of times he'd get up and walk off the plane before he realized it.

The passengers weren't safe, either.

Flying back to St. Louis, there'd be a lot of Blues fans on board. They knew who the players were. They'd talk to us, get autographs…and we'd put shaving cream in their shoes. Or Jean-Guy would take a passenger's hat, a fedora, while he was talking to us and pass it around. The first time Jean-Guy did it he said, "This fan wants you to sign it." So we all signed the fedora and passed it back to Jean-Guy. He put it back in the overhead compartment when the guy wasn't looking.

The other passengers would get a kick out of this, too. They'd sit there watching the shaving cream in the shoes or on the head, or the hat being autographed. We never put shaving cream on anyone we didn't know. If we signed a guy's hat, we always offered to buy a new one if he complained. But nobody ever did. They liked having something different that was autographed.

I was the quiet one. So any time I pulled a joke on anyone—a player or a passenger—I always put the blame on Noel Picard.

I'd say, "I'm not saying anything, but I think I saw Noel with the shaving cream a little while ago."

And we always liked getting Noel whenever we could. One time we got his shoes and put them up front, inside a passenger's carry-on bag underneath the seat.

When the plane landed, Noel jumped up, looked right at me and yelled, "Bobby, where are my shoes!"

I said, "Honest, Noel, I don't have your shoes."

Which was true.

People were leaving the plane and Noel was going crazy, asking everybody for his shoes. Then the guy whose bag they were in was ready to leave.

I said, "Noel, were they brown shoes?"

He said, "You know what color they were!"

I said, "See that guy getting off the plane? I'm sure I saw him put a pair of brown shoes in his overnight bag."

So then Noel knew that we got him. But he was thinking, "Go get that guy!"

By the time Noel could get off the plane, the guy was way down the concourse. Noel was in his socks, so he couldn't really run. But he was walking real fast.

Noel finally caught up to the guy. He put that big hand of his on the guy's shoulder and said, "Pardon me, sir, you've got my shoes."

Now, you've got to appreciate this. Noel was a big strong guy, his English was not the best, and he had that French accent that nobody could understand. The guy had no idea what Noel was talking about. He tried to keep walking. But Noel had his hand on the guy's shoulder, saying, "Sir, sir, you don't understand."

The guy kept trying to get away. Noel was saying, "Sir, please! Those guys over there played a trick on me. They put my shoes in your bag."

What a guy: Jean-Guy Talbot knew when to play hard and when to have fun. *(Bruce Bennett Studios)*

The guy opened the bag, and there were Noel's shoes. The guy had no idea what was going on. Just then we all walked past, and we yelled at the guy, "Thief, thief!"

Waiting Game

You couldn't do any of this stuff now with security the way it is in airports. Plus, the teams all charter everywhere. They get to the airport, the bus pulls right onto the runway, and they board the planes out there. The only time they get inside the terminal is if they're clearing customs in Canada or the States.

But when we flew commercial, we spent an awful lot of time in airports.

Delays, cancellations, mechanical problems, bad weather…you could be waiting for four or five hours for a connection. But it wasn't boring when you had characters around like Noel Picard and Jean-Guy Talbot.

When you stay in those nicer hotels, along with the free soap and shampoo you get these little sewing kits. They're about the size of a matchbook, and they really did come in handy.

Especially on nights when Noel had to stitch up his pants.

The sewing kit had different color threads, which was really handy because the airport would have different color floors or rugs.

You'd pick out a thread that matched the floor. You'd poke it through one end on the paper sleeve that held your ticket, and you'd put a five dollar bill in there that just stuck out of the sleeve. You'd put it on the floor in the concourse and sit about 10 feet away, holding the thread. People would walk by, glance down and see the money sticking out of the ticket sleeve, as if someone had dropped it.

We'd be over in the waiting area, betting on which people would stop. But we'd never stare at them to give it away.

You'd always get someone who would slow down, look around, stop and bend over to pick it up.

And then the money would start hopping away.

The people bending over couldn't see the string being pulled. But the other passengers in the waiting rooms would see what we were doing. It was entertaining for them, too.

Or, four guys would get some big sheets of paper and write a different number on each one, from 1 to 10. When the people would walk by, the guys would hold up a number to rate the girls. Somebody would put up a "5", and we'd go, "Boo, boo!" And he'd quickly put a "9" up, and we'd cheer.

You couldn't do that now, either. It's not politically correct. But nobody seemed to mind back then.

The other thing Noel did was wait for a guy to come by in a hurry with a bag in each hand. Noel would walk by and say, "Pardon me, sir, but your fly is open." And you'd always see the guy swing one bag in front of himself to cover his fly so he could keep walking down the hall.

Noel did that one time to a guy in our hotel lobby. The guy was holding a bag over one shoulder, with a bag in his other hand and a third bag under that arm and two cameras around his neck.

Noel told him his fly was open. So the guy stopped and set the bags down. The cameras were swinging around. The guy checked, and it wasn't open. So he started looking for Noel, found him and started chasing him around the hotel lobby. Noel got out of there and the guy gave up.

Or a guy would be in the locker room reading a paper. All of a sudden, the paper would go up in flames. That one scares the heck out of you, especially because everyone would start yelling, "Hot news, hot news!"

You'd hear that, and you'd know Noel was around.

Shoe Was Fun

You'd be sitting in an airport waiting room, and all of a sudden a guy would jump up and hop around and stomp his foot.

There would be Noel, crawling down between the seats, as big as he is, and reaching with the matches for the hot foot.

That's another one you couldn't do with security now in the airports.

Another thing the guys used to do was make a messy distraction at team dinners. They'd have the bottles of mustard and ketchup on the table, and Frank St. Marseilles or Gary Sabourin would crawl under a table, pouring ketchup on everyone's shoes.

A little while later, you hear, "Shoe check, shoe check!"

You'd say, "Oh, geez!" And you'd look down, and there'd be ketchup all over your shoes.

Or you'd be at a banquet where the head table was raised off the floor. The celebrities sitting up there had their feet right where you walked by. There were always a lot of people up there before the banquet, talking to the celebrities at the head table. Someone would sneak by and put ketchup on their shoes right there under the head table.

Then later on, during the banquet, someone would say to the front table, "Check your shoes, check your shoes!"

Our guys always loved to get any football Cardinals sitting at the head table. We were friends with all those guys.

The thing is, you weren't safe in those days. No matter where you went, something was going to happen. And it was harmless fun.

No Laughing Matter

Noel Picard was a white-knuckle flyer. That's the only time you could shut him up, when a plane hit a bump or had some turbulence.

Big, tough Noel. When we landed, he'd grab that seat in front of him and hold on. We'd say, "Nice landing, Noel!"

Same thing with my brother Barc. He hated to fly, too. He even went out to McDonnell Douglas in St. Louis, and they showed him how strong the planes were put together.

He didn't care. Flying wore him out more than the hockey game did.

When I was in the minors with the Baltimore Clippers, we had to crash the plane in downtown Cleveland once to land. Oh, it was a tough landing. We were coming in, bouncing and everything. Some guys were still not nervous, and they'd joke every time we hit a bump in the air. And I was one of them.

The plane came in for the landing, and it was weaving back and forth, and we'd hit a bump like a roller coaster, and we'd all go, "Ohhhhhhh!"

We got close to the runway, the wheels were down and we were coming in, and all of a sudden, the pilot gunned the plane and it started to climb. Fast!

The wheels went back up like we were going up to make another pass at it. Then the plane went right down again on the runway. And that's when everyone got real quiet. Me too!

This was not a big charter jet. We landed without the wheels down, and we could see the sparks outside the window and the smoke, which was coming inside. The plane went off the runway. The airport in Cleveland was near Lake Erie, and the water was right there. We got off the plane, and nobody was still saying too much. The fire trucks and emergency vehicles were coming. We heard the sirens.

And there was a bus for us. We got on the bus and started driving right away to our hotel. Our coach, Terry Reardon, saw the bus go past a little bar. He was still shook up and he said, "Pull the bus in here!"

We started drinking. We were playing in Cleveland the next night, so normally we wouldn't be out doing that. We were there for a while, and Terry said, "We're not going to the hotel yet."

Then it got to where we were all joking about it. We found out later that this one was close. I mean close. The plane got caught in a downdraft. That's why it started back up from the first landing. Then the downdraft grabbed us and threw us down on the runway before we could get up away from it.

It turned out there was a report on the radio in Baltimore that a plane crashed in Cleveland carrying the Clippers hockey team—but no further news. The wives started calling the hotel to find out if anyone was hurt, and we hadn't checked in yet. We were still at the bar. None of the husbands had called home. Remember, there were no cell phones back then.

So the wives and everyone back in Baltimore thought no one survived the crash. On that plane with me that night was Billy Collins, who later played for the Blues.

So later on, when the Blues would fly and Barc would get scared, I'd say, "Barc, what are the chances of being in a plane crash? One in a million? One in two million?"

Barc would say, "I don't care."

I'd say, "Well, what are the odds of a guy being in two plane crashes? One in 10 million? I've already been in one, so you're safe with me on the plane."

Barc would say, "I don't care."

After Billy Collins came to the Blues in the '73-74 season, I'd say, "Barc, what are the odds that *two* guys that have already crashed together on a plane will crash together *a second time*? One in 50 million? One in 100 million? You're *really* safe with us here."

Barc said, "I still don't care."

He was still very nervous. Every time he flew.

Irish Eyes Unsmiling

Our players were nothing compared to Dan Kelly, our broadcaster. He feared flying. He *hated* flying.

He covered hockey for the Blues and Canadian networks, and then he'd go cover baseball and football and other sports. So he was always in the air.

When he got on our plane, we called him "One Match Dan." One match, one pack of cigarettes. You could smoke on planes then, and he would light that first cigarette as soon as we got in the air. He'd use that one to light the next one, just chain smoke for the whole flight.

He had reasons to be nervous. Hey, try riding in a DC-3 when you get a headwind. It bounces, and sometimes you look at the cars down below and they're going faster than you are.

Dan was more afraid of flying than any of us, but we didn't kid him. He got a little respect because of how great he was—the best hockey broadcaster in the world. And he got respect because when we were in the air, Dan would just tell you to shut up.

Train of Thought

W hen you couldn't fly and the airports were slow, it was either the bus or a train.

In the Blues' third season, we had beaten Toronto at home and then flew to Toronto to play the next night. After we got there, they had a big blizzard all across Canada. It closed the airport in Toronto, and they didn't know when it was going to end.

We lost the game that night, December 27, and then we took the late train to Montreal.

There was a liquor strike going on in Quebec Province. All the liquor stores were closed. We had quite a few players from Montreal on our team, and their families asked if we could bring some liquor in for them.

The team only liked to drink beer, but everybody was bringing as much liquor through customs as we were allowed for the players' families.

We left Toronto about 11:30 p.m. after the game. The Blues had their own sleeper car at the end of the train, with bunks up and down the aisle. Scotty Bowman was the coach, so he had his own compartment at the front of the car. So we sat back there and had our team meetings and our talks and Scotty went up to his compartment.

We had never beaten the Canadiens in our history, but we wouldn't be playing them for three days. So even though we lost in Toronto, we had some beer on the train since there was no game the next day. We finished off the beer, and then a few bottles of the liquor started to come out. Jean-Guy Talbot played the mouth organ—the harmonica—and that came out. We were sitting around singing, and then Jean-Guy started playing "I'm Dreaming of a White Christmas."

Somebody ended up swinging a pillow—a feather pillow. We knew that because it popped open and feathers were everywhere. Pretty soon, everyone started grabbing pillows and swinging them at each other and ripping them open. These white feathers were flying out, and we were throwing them all over the place, and singing that we're dreaming of a white Christmas.

All of a sudden we looked over. And there stood Scotty Bowman, with his black pants and no shirt…covered in feathers…on his black pants, in his hair, on his face.

Jean-Guy was standing up front with his harmonica, facing us, just playing away. He couldn't see Scotty right behind him. Nothing was said, but nobody was singing any more. We started diving into the bunks. Jean-Guy turned around and there was Scotty, covered in feathers.

Scotty didn't say a word. He went back to his compartment. It was quiet for a few minutes. Then the guys came back out and you heard:

"To look sharp, and to feel sharp too
There's a razor that is made for you."

We decided to shave a rookie. They were all sweating, but there was no place for them to go and hide. So we got one and initiated him. And there was all kinds of noise.

Gus Kyle, a former player who was one of our broadcasters, kept yelling that he wanted to go to sleep. Noel told him to shut up and mind his own business. A few words were exchanged. Gus Kyle was tough when he played, but not tougher than Noel Picard. And Noel was very, very mad.

We stepped between them and wouldn't let Noel do anything. Gus went back to bed. That was the end of it. Or so we thought.

We got to Montreal the next day. The cabs weren't running because of the blizzard. Our hotel was just a block away, but we had to walk through snow banks 10-, 15-feet high.

As we got up in the morning on the train, Glenn Hall had no shoes. He had left them at the bottom of his bunk but they were gone. You didn't mess with Glenn Hall. He was the goalie, and he was headed to the Hall of Fame. You never said a word to him on the day of the game. He was so intense, he would throw up before every game. We'd hear him in the bathroom in the locker room, and we'd say, "Okay, Glenn's ready."

Now his shoes were missing on the train. He was yelling, "You immature guys, where are my shoes?"

Nobody could find them. Nobody knew what happened to them. Hey, I didn't do it.

Finally, Noel said, "You know, it's funny. Last night I have a dream that I throw some shoes off the train."

And Jean-Guy said, "You know what? I had a dream that I watched you throw them off."

They were in it together. They thought they were throwing Gus Kyle's shoes off, but they got the wrong pair.

Well, Glenn Hall wouldn't even talk to us. Any of us. Somebody tried to give him some galoshes to wear but he wouldn't take them. He walked all the way from the train to the hotel, through all the snow, in his socks. He didn't want anything to do with us. It didn't matter that his shoes got thrown off the train by mistake.

We had a meeting before practice that day for the next game. And this was great for Scotty.

He had an excuse to tear into us. A lot of excuses. The drinking…the shoes…the pillows…the feathers all over him.

But, we'd had a great party. We broke some rules, but we had a great time. We were together, except for Glenn. We knew we would be a better team afterward. That's where you play guilty.

Scotty came into the meeting with the same pants he wore on the train. You could see a few little feathers here and there on the pants. He started talking. He had his chin in the air and his hands in his pockets, the way he always did, jingling his change. And a feather floated up out of his pocket.

He kept jingling the change, and another feather came out. And another one. And another one. These little feathers were floating around. He didn't see them, but we were trying not to laugh.

Then we went out and skated hard at practice. We did the same thing the next day. The next night, we were ready to play Montreal.

The game started and we never trailed. We were up 1-nothing, 2-nothing, 3-nothing. Glenn Hall still wasn't talking to us, but he was unbelievable. When it hit 4-nothing, this was what makes the fans in Montreal so great. They knew they were not going to win that game. So they cheered every save that Glenn made. And he made a lot of them. They wanted to see him get his shutout. And he did. We won 5-nothing. Glenn was the first star of the game.

Whenever you win, you go up to the goalie and pat him on the head to congratulate him. And he says, "Hey, fellas, way to go." This time after the game, Glenn was dodging all of us, trying to get to the dressing room so he didn't have to talk to us. He kept mumbling, "immature idiots!" He didn't talk to us for a couple of weeks. But for the rest of the season, he'd be sitting in the dressing room, and one of us would walk by and say, "You know, I had a dream last night where I threw my shoes out the bedroom window…"

Purple Snow

In one of the first years of the Blues, on our western swing, we ended up in Squaw Valley, California. Scotty wanted to get the guys together for three or four days late in the season, on a trip when you have a space in the schedule. Just to get everyone's minds off hockey before the playoffs.

That had never been done before. Now teams do it all the time. They'll be on a trip and have a few days off when they're in Florida or California or Phoenix. But there were no West Coast or Southern teams when the NHL just had the Original Six: Montreal, Toronto, Boston, New York, Detroit and Chicago. Then we got the six new teams in the first expansion, and the league had teams in Los Angeles and Oakland along with St. Louis, Minnesota and Philadelphia.

We had three days off on one of those trips to California, and that's when Scotty took us to Squaw Valley. The Winter Olympics had been there in 1960—the U.S. hockey team won the gold medal—but none of us had ever been there. Pulling in on the bus, you couldn't even see some of the houses because of the snowdrifts.

Scotty gave us the first day off. And the second day off, with the ice there for an optional practice. The third day, we had practice and everyone had to be there. Scotty's optional practices weren't really optional for everybody. Certain players should take the day off—the older veterans. But with a lot of us, it was—*Scotty's* option whether we practiced. When we'd have an optional back in St. Louis, you'd see Scotty up there in The Arena, at the door to his office, looking down to see who was at the "optional."

But a lot of us wanted to skate at the optionals. They were a lot of fun. They weren't set up like a regular practice. You play little games among yourselves, pickup games without the coaches. The guys from Eastern Canada would play against Western Canada, or Catholics against Protestants. Sometimes the guys worked their butts off harder than a regular practice. Because adult beverages went to the winners from the losers.

On our Squaw Valley trip, the first day we heard the rumor that Scotty and some friends out there were taking a trip to Reno, Nevada, which wasn't too far away. So we were on our own.

That evening we scouted the different spots around Squaw Valley. There were quite a few people, mostly tourists and skiers. One of the players found a fondue restaurant. That was new then, where you dipped your bread into a pot of cheese, everybody together. But the big thing was, they had the music in that place. People were singing, the players were singing, but we didn't know the music was being piped out into the village.

We got Noel Picard up there with a French song, and Jean-Guy Talbot got up there with him. Then somebody started playing "When The Saints Go Marching In," and we started singing, "When the *Blues* Go Marching In," like our fans did at The Arena.

We found out later that Scotty came back that night and heard this singing out in town and said, "Those are my players!" He was climbing up the snow banks to see where the music was coming from. We weren't in trouble, though. He was happy that we were out together—what's the word now?—bonding.

The next day, we had the optional skate. Again, most of the guys did it. Afterward it was lunch and then we rented snowmobiles. We weren't allowed to ski, because they were afraid we'd get hurt, but we would take the lifts to the top of the hill. They had a big restaurant and a bar there.

It was so sunny up there, and warm. You sat up there outside on a lawn chair and took your shirt off and took in the sights. A few guys had bottles of red wine. You just put the bottles in the snow beside you to chill it.

All of a sudden, somebody said, "Here comes Scotty!"

So you put your bottle all the way down into the snow to hide it. What you didn't know was when the snow got in the top of the bottle, for some reason the wine started to come out. You looked down, and there was all this purple snow by everyone's chair.

Scotty walked past and didn't say a word. He had his head up in the air, as usual, but we knew he saw it.

We just started laughing.

So we had a pretty good day that second day, and another good evening.

Paying the Price

The next day in Squaw Valley, our third day there, was the required practice. We worked hard. And then Scotty ended it up with a skate. No pucks, just skating.

It was a marathon skate. Some guys were excused, older guys like Red Berenson and Al Arbour. But the rest of us were up and down, up and down.

After awhile, Scotty would pick a couple older guys and tell them, "One more good one up and down, and then off." So those guys would finish up and leave. Scotty would pick another couple guys, same thing.

Then it was just the younger guys left, and Scotty wasn't sending any of us off early. He said, "You're all going to go until you can go no more." He wanted to make us quit. So it was up and down, up and down, with Scotty yelling, "Pick it up, pick it up!" It was push and glide, push and glide, and you bent over so you could get your breath. The elevation up there was why it was so tough on us, not just what we did the night before.

Pretty soon guys started to drop out and leaned over the boards. And some of what we did the last night was going over the boards, if you know what I mean.

I kept going up and down, but I was going so slow. Everybody else was going as hard as they could. And then I was the last guy skating.

Scotty started yelling, "Speed it up, Plager, speed it up!"

I said, "This is as fast as I can go, Scotty, and I can go all day. You'll never make me quit!"

I went up the ice and touched the endboards. And when I turned around to come back, he was already gone.

The whole thing up there in Squaw Valley was such a great experience. When we left for our games in Los Angeles and Oakland, we were ready. We played hard and we won. That was part of Scotty's thinking about taking us to Squaw Valley. He knew we wanted to do it again. We knew that if we played good, we'd probably come back. And we did for the next couple years.

And in all our times out there, we never lost a game on the West Coast. Now you look back and you think, "Geez, it was the bonding."

And that was Scotty. You look back at a lot of his thoughts, and you see that a lot of coaches now put a lot of Scotty in their own coaching.

Off-season Non-training

Players today all have the personal trainers, and work out year-round. Training camps in our day needed to be a month long. We played 13 exhibition games, twice as many as they have now. You went to camp to get in shape. Now the players report and they're already in great shape.

That's because we all worked regular jobs in the summer time. We never made money then playing hockey, so you didn't have the time to work out all day in the offseason.

The most I ever made was $65,000 in my last year, 1977-78. We didn't have multi-year contracts then. The contracts were year to year.

In '64, when I signed my first pro contract with the New York Rangers, Emile Francis was the general manager. You walked in his office and you didn't negotiate. You took what they offered or you went home—unless you were a superstar—then you had some argument.

When I walked in that first time, Emile said, "You're not that far away from the NHL. If you make the team, we'll give you $7,500."

Then he said, "But if you play at our number one farm club in Baltimore in the American Hockey League, you'll make $5,500."

That still wasn't too bad. Then he said, "Here's what you get if you go to St. Paul in the International Hockey League: $5,000."

So it was a three-way contract. But he kept pointing at the NHL contract and saying how close I was to making the Rangers. Of course the next year I'm at St. Paul and making five grand, the lowest salary.

But I saved my money and I bought a used car. In the off season, I went back home to Ontario and got a job at a brewery in Kapuskasing, about 120 miles north of Kirkland Lake. The place I worked at was really like a warehouse. The beer was all sent by train up there. I filled the beer orders for the hotels. Which means I worked on the beer truck—delivering, unloading, and stocking the beer.

When I went to the Rangers, they did a little story for the program. They asked me, "What do you do for the summer?"

I said, "I'm a beer taster. I go to the different hotels and the bars, and if I say the beer's no good they've got to throw it out."

The story hit all the papers. And the brewery was swamped with everybody applying for jobs. They all wanted to be beer tasters. The brewery had to write letters to all the papers, saying, "There is no such job as a beer taster. What Bob Plager does is deliver the beer on the truck."

Hey, all I tried to do was explain to the writer that I wasn't going to deliver bad beer. So I had to taste it first, right?

Conditioning Tips

I look now at a guy like Al MacInnis of the Blues. He's 40 years old and in better shape than these kids who come to camp.

Not me. Every year I'd go to training camp a little overweight. I'm five-foot-10 and I played at a little more than 200 pounds. At the end of the season, I'd be down to 198, 197. My brother Barc lost a lot more weight every season. He'd come in to camp about 188 and end up about 168. When Barc got his letter about camp, it would say: "Report at as much as you want." He'd be eating all summer and still not be higher than 186, 188.

I'd come into camp at 212, 214 pounds. My second year in St. Louis, the letter came from Scotty after the season: "Report at 196 pounds." I'd never been that low. I phoned Scotty and said, "You've got me coming to camp lower than what I finished the season."

I thought it was a mistake. Scotty just said, "I know what I put in there."

I went out and had my usual summer up in Ontario anyway. I came back to St. Louis two weeks before we left for camp and I was about 220.

It would be 90-some degrees in St. Louis and real humid. I would put on my long underwear, my rubber sweat pants and sweat jacket, get in my car, roll the windows up and drive around with the heater on.

That was dumb. You can get heat stroke doing that. It's a wonder I didn't, because I was soaking wet when I'd get out of the car. Then I'd get on the water pills and lose the rest of my water that I hadn't sweated out.

I wouldn't eat. I quit drinking beer. I was scared. I had to go and weigh in that first day. And I wasn't the only player like that. Noel Picard would always be a few pounds over.

The team was meeting in Ottawa to check in, have the physicals, and weigh in. Then we were going to St. Andrews, New Brunswick, for training camp. We were in Ottawa the night before the official weigh-in, and Noel was drinking grapefruit juice. He hadn't eaten in about 10 days to get his weight down.

That night, I went into the bathroom and shut the door and put a towel underneath it. I turned on the hot water in the shower and sat on the floor, trying to steam off some last extra pounds.

The next morning we had the weigh-in. Everybody who'd seen me during the summer was waiting for me to get on the scale. In those days the only thing they cared about was your weight. Today the players are checked for their body fat, and they have to do repetitions lifting weights, and all of that. I couldn't have passed any of those tests. I was weak and dizzy from dropping all that weight so fast.

Scotty was there by the scale. Cliff Fletcher, who was helping Scotty, was there.

Noel got on, and he was just about where he was supposed to weigh. Barc got on, and he was in the 180s.

Then Scotty said, "Okay, Bob, get on."

I got on the scale, and it was…1…9…6.

Right away, Scotty said, "Off the scale!"

He adjusted it a little bit and said, "Okay, back on. Put one foot on, and then the other foot."

I was grinning, because I didn't cheat the first time. I got on again. Same thing—196.

Scotty said to Tommy Woodcock, the trainer, "What's the matter with this thing?"

Tommy said, "Nothing. That's what he weighs." And he wrote 196 on my chart.

After we got our medicals, we had a little get together. We were leaving the next morning for camp at St. Andrews, so we found a nice little night spot in Ottawa. I hadn't eaten all day. I hadn't had a drink in days. So the pitchers of beer started to come. There were some pickled eggs there at the bar. On the way back to the hotel there was a fried chicken place, and I bought a bucket of chicken. Family size. I took the chicken up to my room, pulled a waste basket over to the bed, turned on the TV, got on the bed and shoved the whole bucket of chicken down my throat. That waste basket was filled with bones.

The next morning I got up and had a big breakfast. Then it was off to St. Andrews. We had a golf tournament in the afternoon, a planned event with lots of beverages on the course.

The lunch was pretty good out there. And after the golf tournament, they had a banquet. St. Andrews is known for its lobster. We had all we could eat, with melted butter, and washed it down with more beer.

The next day Scotty called for us to weigh in at the practice. I was…2…0…9.

I'd put on 13 pounds in two days! After practice, I was walking by when Scotty checked the weights. He didn't see me, and he was yelling at Tommy Woodcock, "Is this right for Bob Plager?"

I walked past Scotty, tapped him on the shoulder and said:

"Scotty, the letter said *report* at 196. It didn't say *stay* there."

But I wasn't worried about it. We would lose four or five pounds a day at camp. Scotty worked us hard, and we started to eat right.

What helped later on was when Barc and I took up tennis. We weren't great, but we could lob the ball over the net and run after it.

A couple weeks before camp, I would still ride around the car with the windows up and the heat on. But about four years into it in St. Louis, the letter after the season said: "Training camp is to make the hockey club, not to get in shape."

So I started reporting at not much more than 200 pounds.

Whoa, Nellie!

John Davidson came here as a 20-year-old rookie goaltender. His second year here, 1974-75, he bought Glen Sather's house on Wild Horse Creek Road way out in Chesterfield Valley after Glen got traded. It was a big house and five acres. With the house came a horse, a Tennessee Walker.

John was a newlywed, and one night he had a party out at the house for all the players. During the party, Floyd Thomson and I went out to see the horse. Floyd took his belt off and put it around the horse's neck, and we brought the horse up to the house.

I got on the horse and Floyd opened the front door. I was going to ride the horse into the house, but I forgot to duck going through the door. I hit my head and fell off.

The horse continued into the house and started sliding on the hardwood floors. The people inside panicked and then the horse panicked. It got into one of the rooms that had a nice new white carpet. It kicked and left dents in the walls, and it left mudprints all over the white carpet.

They finally got the horse back outside. Like anything else, at the time we thought it was really funny. The next day in the dressing room, John explained how funny it wasn't.

His wife was still screaming about it.

Hunting Snipe

R ed Berenson knew the Wallach brothers, who lived out in Eureka, about a half-hour drive outside of St. Louis. They owned acres out there in the country.

One of the first years with the Blues, one of the guys who had played in Montreal said to Red, "You've got to arrange a snipe hunt with your buddies out there."

A couple of days later, Jean-Guy Talbot said, "Did you ask your buddies if we could hunt snipe?"

Red said, "Yep, and they're running good."

Jean-Guy said, "Okay, let's pick up sides."

We made two teams and were sure to have two rookies on one team.

One of the young guys said, "What are snipe?"

Red said, "They're small birds that come out at night and always run to a light. So we turn on a big spotlight and we hunt them with a big fish net.

"You catch them and just throw them into a burlap sack. They're really quick. So you've got to be fast because they will really be coming."

Red had a lot of people involved. They had the holding cells set up and the courthouse all ready in Eureka. Then we met a place called Joe Boccardi's Ristorante. We had people at Boccardi's telling the two rookies, "Here's how you throw the snipe out of the net and into the sack. You bring 'em back here, and we'll kill 'em and clean 'em. But we just take the breast."

The restaurant had some kind of spaghetti sauce, and the guy said, "This is what we put 'em in. It's the best snipe sauce you ever tasted."

Then we all went out to the property that Red's buddies owned, this cornfield that was all cut down. We had two floodlights, one on each end of the field. The two rookies were at one end with their net and their sack.

We told them, "We'll go out in the field and make noise. That's when the snipe will all be coming, so get ready."

We all walked off and yelled for about 20 seconds. That's when the game wardens came driving up with their red light going. They walked up to the two rookies and said, "What's going on here?"

The kids said, "We're hunting snipe."

The wardens said, "Well, it's out of season. Who gave you permission to hunt here?"

The kids said, "Red's friends."

They had no clue what the name was.

The wardens said, "Where's your permit?"

The kids said, "We don't have one. Red and the guys said it was okay."

So they got arrested. The wardens put handcuffs on them and took them in the squad car to the holding cell.

We got in our cars and followed them, just laughing. Red and some guys went in and told the rookies, "We can't bail you out yet. The judge is coming. Geez, you two could lose your visa over this. They could ship you back to Canada. Your careers could be over."

Meanwhile, the rest of the team was over at Joe Boccardi's, having a drink and a great time.

Then it was time to go to the courtroom. We were sitting there with beer under the benches. The wardens brought the two kids in, and one of the Eureka guys said, "Here come da judge!" Just like in the old *Laugh-In* comedy show.

The two kids still didn't get it.

The judge was Buzz Westfall. He was the prosecuting attorney for St. Louis County back then, and now he's the County Executive. Westfall started reading off the charges. The two rookies didn't have a lawyer, so Red was defending them.

Westfall said, "On the charge of hunting out of season, how do you plead, guilty or not guilty?"

The kids looked at Red, and he just shrugged his shoulders. So they said, "Guilty."

Westfall said, "To the charge of trespassing, how do you plead?"

Red said, "Well, we did have permission."

Westfall said, "Who gave you permission?"

One of the brothers stood up and said, "I did!" And the other brother stood up and said, "You did what?" And they started arguing. The one who gave the permission was pretending to be drunk, and it looked like they were ready to fight.

Westfall said, "Well, if you don't agree on the permission, I guess it's guilty on that one."

Everything was guilty, and we had them convinced they would lose their visas. Then Westfall said, "The fine is $1,700."

Of course the kids don't have $1,700. Somebody started to write a check, and one of the policemen tore it up and said, "We don't take checks."

So they hauled the two kids back to the cells, and we all went back to Joe Boccardi's. We let them sit in jail for a while. Then we went and told them we got enough cash to pay the fine.

The two kids never did catch on, so we had to tell them.

We did the snipe hunts for years and years. Young Sid Salomon got involved. So did Scotty Bowman, and so did Al Arbour when he was the coach.

One year when the two rookies got caught, we had them phone Al to say, "We don't have the bail money."

Al told them, "I don't care. You just get your own bail money. And you better be at practice tomorrow. Or whatever you got fined there, it'll be double up here!"

The year they got Brian Sutter and Bernie Federko, it was very hard to convince them the snipe hunt was real. They weren't sure it was a joke, but they didn't bite as hard as some of the others did.

The guys who got fooled always thought it was funny. Except Chuck Lefley. He was caught, and he was by himself because he was the only rookie. He went to the court and put up a big argument. I think he was fined $2,000.

When it was all over, he came out and the guy playing the judge tapped him on the shoulder and said, "No hard feelings?"

Chuck started yelling, "You just fined me $2,000, and you've got the nerve to say no hard feelings?"

The judge looked at us and said, "Haven't you told him yet?"

When Chuck was told, he didn't think it was too funny.

Snipe Extinction

We didn't want the young players to know there were no such thing as snipes. But it got tougher and tougher. One of the St. Louis writers put it in the newspaper and the word started getting out.

But it was always a big thing in Eureka. The people there got into it big time. We'd drive through that night, and the townspeople would say, "Oh, are you going to the snipe hunt?" Every year, the same two guys from town would show the rookies how to use the net and the gunney sack. Then the same guy at Joe Boccardi's would take the kids into the kitchen to see the special sauce. Then we'd take them out to that same field, and we'd see that red light coming down that dirt road, and go through the whole thing, with the two brothers arguing in the court.

It was always a great time. It brought the team together. You'd party, and then you'd skate hard the next day.

In the spring of '85, they set up the snipe hunt the way they always did. I wasn't there. Frankie Burns, the Blues equipment manager, had this half-ton pickup truck that he parked in Eureka for the hunt. Doug Wickenheiser had come over from Montreal a couple of years before. He had some buddies down from Canada, and they were all in on it.

Guys were coming out of Boccardi's to head out for the hunt. They were piling into the back of Frankie's truck, and Wick tried to jump up into the bed. He didn't make it. He kind of fell back, and stepped back and tried again. He fell back again and stepped back into the street as he came down. It was just a two-lane street. A car drove by and clipped Wick and ripped his knee up.

Wick was in pain, but he was peeved that he was going to miss the hunt. He told the guys, "Just go ahead."

He didn't realize how bad his knee was torn up. Jerry Gilden, our orthopedic surgeon, did a great job with the operation. They asked Doc Gilden if Wick would ever play again. But when he saw the x-rays, he said, "Never mind that. The question is, will Wick ever walk properly again?"

Wick went through a lot of tough rehab after that. He was supposed to be out for two years at least. He came back in about nine months.

But that was the end of the snipe hunts.

Even though I wasn't there when Wick got hurt, I heard about it from Ron Caron, who had come from Montreal to be the general manager.

Ron was yelling, "St. Louis is too much of a fun place. What are they doing out there? What is this snipe hunt?"

I said, "Ron, this has been going on for years. It's a tradition and the guys love it…and it came from Montreal."

Doc Gilden

Wick worked so hard on his rehab. I'd see him down there at the old Arena, by himself, and we didn't have the best equipment then or these personal trainers that they have now.

But Jerry Gilden did an unbelievable job on the surgery. Just like he did when he put Noel Picard's ankle back together.

Noel was riding a horse, a young horse. It got spooked and it bucked and it fell right down on Noel. He got up to walk away, and his leg bone was sticking through his ankle. He was wearing cowboy boots, and his ankle was turned backwards.

Noel had to crawl to a farmhouse to get help. It took the ambulance about 20 to 25 minutes to get there. Jimmy Roberts was called down to the hospital. Barc was there, and Vivian, Noel's wife, was there.

Doc Gilden had examined Noel and they had a blanket over his foot. They'd had to cut the boot off.

Vivian said, "He'll miss the whole year, won't he?"

Doc Gilden said, "He might not play hockey again. We might have to take his foot off."

It had turned black from no blood going to it all that time. Doc Gilden said that if Noel wasn't an athlete, he wouldn't have even tried to save the foot. But he operated and he placed the bone back. Then he ran a blood vessel outside the foot to get blood back to the toes.

If the blood got through, it would make the foot pink again and everything would be okay. Doc Gilden told Noel that if the color wasn't back and he couldn't wiggle his toes, the foot would have to come off. But, the foot changed color and the toes were wiggling, and Noel was back that season.

By the way, Doc Gilden and Aaron Birenbaum, our great doctor of internal medicine, are the only Blues people besides me who have been with the team since it started.

Measuring Toughness

Being on the ice with Noel, I felt like I was six-foot-four, 230 pounds, instead of five-foot-10, 200 pounds.

Somebody would be running around on the other team, and I'd say to Noel on the bench, "I'm going to go get that guy."

Noel would say, "I'll be right there with you."

When I was on defense with Noel, I could play my game, throw my body checks, run guys, clear the front of the net and not worry about somebody jumping me. I loved playing with him, and he loved playing with me. But he really loved my brother Barclay.

Barclay was five-foot-11 and 188 pounds, but like I said, he was in the 160s when the season was over. Barc's first year he only played 49 games, yet he led the NHL in penalty minutes. And he only had 153. That's half of what these tough guys get now.

They didn't call penalties then the way they do now. There were no 10-minute misconducts. We left the bench to fight, there would be brawls, and half the time they'd only give two or three penalties. That's why I only have 802 career penalty minutes in 11 years, and Noel had only 616 in seven years. They just didn't send you to the box that much.

The change came in with Philadelphia, with that Dave Schultz and the Broad Street Bullies. The penalties started going up then. Schultz and guys like Tiger Williams, their penalties were unbelievable.

Before that, the skilled players stood up for themselves. Guys like Gordie Howe, Rocket Richard, Ted Lindsay,

Dickie Moore and Henri Richard. Pound for pound, there wasn't anybody tougher than Henri Richard.

The tough guys could play back then. John Ferguson Sr. was tough, but he went up and down and played the game. He was a better player than Schultz—way better. The same with Noel Picard.

Then they started bringing in the crazy guys in the '70s. That's when the Broad Street Bullies came in.

And the game was changing with all the penalty minutes.

Having a goon time: Big guys like Dave Schultz (right) of the Broad Street Bullies started the penalty-minute craze in the '70s. *(Bruce Bennett Studios)*

Gasser

Charles Catto was the Blues' general manager when we came to training camp in '73. That's when we started having a rookie camp. It was in St. Louis. John Wensink was there. Schultz's brother, Ray, was there. And Bob Gassoff was there. Barc and I had heard of those three, and there were other kids they brought in. All big, tough guys.

The veterans didn't go on the ice in rookie camp. But those of us who lived in town would go down to The Arena, use our sauna and whirlpool, and watch the rookies.

Catto came by and said to my brother and me, "We've got a guy in here who'll take the Plagers."

This is our GM talking. We said, "What?"

Catto said, "It's that guy over there, the one with the scars."

He was talking about some guy nobody knew.

Barc said to Catto, "Why didn't you invite the guy who gave him the scars?"

These tough young guys came into the locker room after the rookie practice, and they were huge. They looked at us and one of them said, "Who are those guys?"

Someone said, "The Plager brothers."

One of the young players said, "*Those* little guys?"

I heard that and I said to Barc, "I think we're going to have a tough training camp!"

Because that rookie camp was all fights. I don't think there was a goal scorer out there.

Then we started training camp for the whole team. Bob Gassoff was there the first day of practice. I'd been introduced to him and he was in our group of defensemen. After the day was over, the veterans usually went to lunch themselves. We didn't hang around with the young guys too much in camp.

But I said, "Bob, you want to come out with us to lunch?"

And then it was, "Bob, you want to come out with us for a few beers tonight?"

And then he was "Gasser." We all liked him right away, because he was tough. I mean, he was *tough*. He feared nobody.

He couldn't play at first. He didn't make the team out of training camp. When he went down to the minors, the word came back: "He's a little bit crazy, too."

Then we called him up, and his first NHL game was in Pittsburgh. We had just made a big trade with them on January 17, 1974. We sent Pittsburgh Steve Durbano, who was very tough and very crazy, and Battleship Kelly, who was as tough as anybody pound for pound, and Ab Demarco, who was not a scrapper. And we got Bugsy Watson, who was a pest, and Greg Polis, a goal scorer, and a draft choice that became Bobby Hess.

You wonder why we gave up all that toughness?

Bob Gassoff. Blues management saw what he could do in the minors. It was time to give him a chance in the NHL.

So six days after the trade, Gasser played his first game. And it was in Pittsburgh. Of course, Durbie and Battleship realized that they got traded because of this kid. So, Durbie took his stick and went after Gasser. And Gasser dropped the gloves and beat him. And beat him. And knocked some of Durbie's teeth right out.

Battleship came right over to Gassoff. It was logical back then to go from one fight to the other. And Gasser took care of Battleship.

Gasser won everything that night. He just showed them how tough he really was. And this is a kid who was just five-foot-11 and 190 pounds, about the same size as me.

It says in the record book that we lost the game 4-1 that night. I don't remember that. But I remember the fights that Bob Gasser had in his first NHL game.

Polished Just Enough

When I was a young player, Doug Harvey told me, "Always remember what got you here. Don't change what got you here. But if you want to stay here, there are a lot of things you have to improve."

In those days, you could break your stick over someone's ankle and get two minutes in the box, or not get a penalty at all. Now you'd get a major penalty and maybe get fined and suspended.

But there was no film then. There was no videotape. No four-game suspensions.

So my advice to Bob Gassoff was, "If they take the puck from you, run them into the corner. If they go around you, whack them with your stick. And you tell them, 'Don't take the puck off me…don't go around me on defense.'"

Pretty soon, you started to see it. Nobody beat him one on one. Nobody ran him into the boards. When he had the puck, he had a lot of room.

And his skills got better. His skating was better. He would work. He was still tough, but his penalties didn't hurt the hockey team.

Off the ice, Gasser was like a little kid, grinning and wanting to have fun with the boys. But he would stand up for the players there, too. There are always people who want to start something with hockey players away from the rink.

Gasser was never looking for anything, but he was always ready for anything. He was a great teammate.

A Tragic Ride

After the '77 playoffs we had a team party on Memorial Day at Garry Unger's farm outside St. Louis. He was having a big pig roast. The players and their families and some of Ungie's neighbors were there. He had horses out there. He had go-karts and dirt bikes, and the kids and everyone were riding around.

Gasser and I had been driving around the property, and when we got back someone had just gotten off a dirt bike. Bob knew how to ride one, so he hopped on one. Bruce Affleck got on one, and a young kid whose dad was a friend of Ungie's got on one.

They all took off and went off the property and down one of those country roads. It was maybe 18 feet wide, with a little hill and another little hill. They went down the road and turned around to come back.

Some young guy at the party had gone to pick up something for Ungie, and he was driving down the road. When he came to this little hill, he almost hit the kid on the dirt bike who came over the top. Then Bruce came over the hill, and the kid in the car almost hit him, too. What they think happened was the kid in the car turned to look at Bruce, and the car hit Bob when he came over the hill.

I was back at the party sitting with Bob's wife Diane, who was pregnant with their first baby. All of a sudden, it was getting quieter and quieter, and then Ungie called me into the house.

Ungie said, "Bob's been in an accident. And it's bad."

Bob's wife came in. She knew something was wrong, but nobody knew exactly what. So she and I and a friend of Bob's got in a truck. We went down the road and a policeman was at the scene of the accident. All he told us was that Bob was taken to the hospital in Washington, Missouri, not too far away.

Then when we got to the hospital, that's when we found out that Bob was dead. He had just turned 24. And there was his wife, pregnant with their first child.

Barc told her, "Don't you worry. When you have your baby, I'll be there with you and my brother Bobby will be there."

Then one night, Barc got the call, and he called me: "Bob, let's go, Diane's having the baby."

We went to Barnes Hospital and she was in labor. Somebody had to go in with her, and it was Barc. I waited outside.

She had little Bobby, and what a great kid he is. Smart, polite, fun to be around.

Diane married Steve Loehr, and what a great guy he is and what a great stepdad. I think Bob would be happy that Diane met someone like Steve.

Little Bobby eventually came down to The Arena and was a stick boy for a couple years. He was a hockey player, a defenseman like his dad. He went to the University of Michigan to play for Red Berenson, and they went to the Final Four and won the national championship.

Bobby had his toughness and his heart—but he was a good player, too. Just like his dad.

"Gasser:" Bob Gassoff made room on the ice the hard way—by pounding it out. *(Bruce Bennett Studios)*

And now he's out in San Diego, training to be a Navy SEAL.

And you know his dad is proud.

Goal Scorer

I wasn't a goal scorer. I had 20 goals in 615 games with the Blues. But I hoped to get one or even two a year.

If you look around, there were a lot of defensemen back then who didn't have 20 goals for a career. Bobby Orr changed all that. Scoring goals wasn't our job until he came in.

One time, when Jean-Guy Talbot was coaching the Blues, I got two goals on one shift. It was against the Rangers here in St. Louis. Gilles Villemure was their goalie, and I had played with him in the minors when we were both Rangers prospects. I had the puck at the point and I just put it on net. I didn't have the hardest shot, but the puck went along the ice. Villemure was screened and it went right in. I put the hands up and celebrated like everyone did.

That was at the beginning of a shift, so I stayed out there. We had the faceoff at center ice. We played for a bit, and then we got the puck in their end again. This time it came back to me at the blue line. I was more or less in the center of the ice. I just flipped the puck backhanded at the net, just hoping for a tip or something.

We had traffic in front of Villemure again. Somebody put up a stick to tip the puck, and Villemure was distracted. The puck was moving so slow. It wasn't a shot you shoot to score.

But it went in.

This time, as soon as I saw the puck in the net, I didn't put my hands up or anything. Everybody came over to congratulate me, but I didn't wait for anyone. I skated as fast as I could to the bench, jumped over the boards and sat down.

Jean-Guy came over and said, "What's the matter? What are you doing?"

I said, "Guy, get me off the ice. They're going to want four from me this year!"

The most I ever had was four goals in a season. But I had two in one game another time. It was in Philadelphia, and I was really trying for that third one.

After I scored the two on the same shift against the Rangers, the next time we went to New York, I was lined up for a faceoff inside the blue line by their bench.

I heard this voice going, "Bobby, Bobby, Bobby!"

It was Gilles Villemure. He wasn't playing that night.

He yelled, "See what happens? You score two goals against me and I get the bench."

And I said, "Gilles, if I score two goals against anybody, he shouldn't even be in the league!"

The Refs

We didn't like the referees in the old days. We thought they were terrible. Hey, they were all great guys, and I know refereeing is tough. But we'd complain when we didn't like a call.

Watching the referees now, I didn't realize how good they were when we played. The referees back then felt the players were going to win or lose the game, not the referee making a call.

They all understood the rivalries and the situations in the game. They would always talk to you, which is good. You could say anything to them, call them anything, and not get a penalty. Now it's unsportsmanlike conduct and two minutes in the box.

We had a game once, a one-goal game in the third period, with John Ashley the referee. Barclay, in front of the net, chopped one of the other players hard across the ankles. It wasn't serious. The player limped a little bit. That's all. Ashley saw the slash but turned his head back up the ice to follow the play.

He figured, "Let the players decide it."

The other player chased up the ice and whacked Barc on the back of the leg with his stick. Ashley saw that, too, and turned his head again. He figured they had settled it and canceled each other out.

The first stoppage after that, Barc went right over to Ashley and yelled, "You saw him slash me!"

Ashley's answer was really serious: "Gee, it's a two-minute penalty for slashing. That's terrible."

Then Ashley had the grin on his face. He said, "Barc, get out of here. I saw you slash him first."

Barc just laughed and skated away.

That's how the referees were then. Yeah, certain referees called more penalties than others. Some referees wanted to come out in the first 10 minutes of a game and take control. But they understood the game. They understood when it was a close game. They knew when the players took care of it themselves. They knew what happened the night before, especially when there were only six teams or even 12 teams.

You saw the same teams all the time, and you saw the same referees all the time. Everybody knew everybody. And you knew how the referees called the game.

Trash-talking Etiquette

You can't talk to the referees now unless you're a captain. In our day, all of the players could talk to the referees. And the referees talked to the players, on the ice and on the bench.

If a referee made a call you didn't like, a *lot* of talk would be going on at the faceoffs. But you kept your head down, and he kept his head down when he was talking to you. That way, you didn't show each other up.

Nobody outside of the faceoff knew you were talking to each other.

Bill Friday was a referee like Paul Stewart, who just retired. Bill did a little showboating out there like Stewie did.

One time, Bill called a penalty on me. I skated by with my head down on the way to the box, and I said, "Bill, that was the stupidest penalty I've ever seen."

Bill had his head down, too, and he said, "Bob, that was the stupidest play I've ever seen."

I got so mad I threw one of my gloves up in the air. Bill said, "If it hits the ice, you've got 10."

Meaning a 10-minute misconduct to go with the two-minute penalty I already had. So I took two strides and caught the glove just before it hit the ice.

Bill skated by and said, "Nice catch!"

The referee back then let the players play, but at times it would get out of hand. Then the referee would come to both benches and say: "I've let them get away with a lot, and I've let you guys get away with a lot. You're both taking advantage. So the next player on either team who breaks a rule is going to the box."

You were warned. And everybody went back to playing hockey.

"Pic" a Seat

In Boston one time, Noel Picard and I were killing a penalty. The Bruins had that great power play: Bobby Orr, Phil Esposito, Johnny Bucyk, Wayne Cashman, Dave Hodge. They were in our end the whole two minutes.

We couldn't get off the ice to change. We were going down to block shots, running around, chasing the puck.

I was so tired I almost said, "Score a goal so we can get out of here."

Then "Pic"—Noel Picard—slid into the boards and fell on top of the puck and we finally got a whistle so we could change players. At Boston, the benches were on opposite sides of the ice. Noel was so tired, he skated over toward the Boston bench.

I didn't think anything about it. The penalty box was there, and I thought he got a delay-of-game penalty for covering the puck.

But Noel went over to the Boston bench, and the Boston guys opened the door. The only ramp to the dressing rooms was by their bench, so I thought he got a misconduct for saying something to the referee.

But Noel was so tired he actually just sat down on the Boston bench. The players slid down to make room. The whole rink was cheering and laughing. Noel had his head down but he heard the noise. He looked over to the side, and all the Boston guys were looking at him and laughing.

Finally there was another stoppage. The referee and the whole rink were staring at poor Noel. He got up, opened the door and skated across the ice to our bench. His head was down. People were cheering. He was red as a beet. That had to be the most embarrassing thing, but as he got to our bench he put his hand up and gave a little wave.

After that, the word was out around the league. We went to Pittsburgh, and one of their players painted a sign behind our bench: *Noel Picard, This Is Your Bench*.

Later on a banquet in St. Louis, Dan Kelly said, "It's good to see Noel Picard in the right city."

Poor Pic. He didn't live that down for a *long* time.

The first (and only) Noel: My partner was always smiling, except when Scotty was around or somebody bothered one of our players. *(Bruce Bennett Studios)*

Sid "ta Turd"

Noel Picard was loved in St. Louis. After he quit playing in '73, he was a broadcaster with Dan Kelly, analyzing the Blues games.

Between periods at home, we would go down to the little room near the dressing room where Frankie Burns had a radio, and we'd listen to Noel analyze what had happened. He worked really hard, and he was really good, but he butchered some things because his English wasn't the greatest.

Sid Salomon the Third wanted to send him to Berlitz, the language school, to help him out. But Mr. Salomon, Sid's dad, said, "Hey, the people love him the way he is. Leave him alone."

Like a lot of French people, Noel said "th" like "t." He couldn't say "third." He would say, "My guest in ta turd period is Sid ta Turd."

Obviously, Young Sid didn't like that. He'd say to Noel, "Quit saying Sid ta Turd."

So the next time they did an interview together, Noel said, "My guest is Sid Two Plus One."

Some of us got Noel to practice saying "third." He worked on it and worked on it and he got it down pretty good.

The next time he got back on the air, he said, "We're ready to start the *thhhird* period…and the score is tied *tree-tree!*"

Time to Go

I retired after the '76-77 season. I was 34 years old, and that was old in those days. You didn't normally play till you were 40 then. Some older guys were brought in when the Blues started, but most of them weren't in the NHL at the time. Doug Harvey was finishing up as a player-coach in the minors. Al Arbour was in the minors and ready to retire. Dickie Moore was retired when Scotty talked him out of it. Those guys were the exceptions, not the rule.

I'd had a bad injury near the end of the previous season. I hit Bryan Trottier of the Islanders with the hip check. He saw me at the last minute and brought his knee up to protect himself. It wasn't dirty. It was a reaction. But he got me right in the side. They took me to the hospital that night on Long Island, and I couldn't breathe, I couldn't laugh, I couldn't cough.

They had to cut my equipment off of me. It hurt too much to try to take it off. The tests showed broken ribs, a bruised kidney and a bruised spleen.

I spent like four days in the hospital there. Al Arbour was coaching the Islanders then, and he came to see me and make sure I was taken care of. When I got out, he had someone from their office pick me up and take me to the airport.

I came back and played at the end of the season and in the playoffs. I taped the ribs but I was still not right. I was still bothered by them all summer. But I had started to work with Teddy Koplar, who owned Channel 11 in St. Louis.

Al Hrabosky, the Cardinals' reliever, did the sports in the winter when baseball was over. When Al played ball in the summer, I did the sports part-time. I was a reporter who went around and interviewed people.

I enjoyed it. I had a lot of fun. Then our sports director was released. I went behind the desk at night but it was just a summertime job, like Al's was a wintertime job. I was still planning to play hockey that fall. Teddy Koplar said, "Well, when you do retire, you'll have a job here."

We went to training camp in Michigan that year. The first couple of practices, I knew my ribs were still acting up. After five days, I wasn't having a good camp. I went in and talked to Emile Francis, our general manager, and told him I was retiring.

Emile said, "Are you sure?"

I said, "I'm sure. I can go work for Channel 11."

Emile said, "Maybe you can come and work for the Blues, too, and do some special assignments for us."

The next morning, we flew back to St. Louis and they announced my retirement.

I don't know if it was a tough decision. I wasn't healthy. Barclay had retired and was coaching our minor league team, which had moved to Kansas City. Bob Gassoff had died that summer, and it was really hard not having him there.

Plus, we had a lot of young players, and it was time for them to get their chance. I thought the team would have a hard time, that there'd be a lot of booing, and I hadn't been booed in St. Louis. I always said I wanted to leave on a good note.

So it was time to go. I hung up my skates and went to Channel 11.

The Unretiring Type

On Thanksgiving of that year, 1977, I had just come back from deer hunting and was home with my family for dinner. The phone rang. It was Emile Francis. He said, "Bob, how's the weight?"

I said, "This turkey dinner I just had must have put on about five pounds."

He said, "Would you be interested in coming back to play?"

I said, "What time's practice tomorrow?"

Believe me, when you get out of it for a while, you do miss it.

The team was going out of town the next day, Friday, and coming back Monday. Emile said, "The ice is yours.

Work out by yourself till the team comes back and we'll make an announcement. Do you think you could play by their first game back on Wednesday?"

I said, "I've been off skates for so long…when is the next game after that?"

He said, "Saturday."

I said, "I'll be ready Saturday."

That first game was against the Islanders, the same team where I'd hurt my ribs my last season. I'd been off skates for seven months except for those five days of camp, and I didn't want to look stupid.

I came out and I got a great ovation. It was probably one of the best games I ever played. I blocked the shots and did a lot of hitting. I threw the hip check where the guy flipped over me. The adrenaline was flowing.

At the end of the game, I felt great. Nothing bothered me. But as the next game came on, I couldn't bounce back. I was tired. I was sore.

I told Emile, "I just don't have it any more."

He said, "Keep going. We'll see how it goes."

But I didn't want to hurt the hockey team. We were struggling anyhow. Then one day at the rink for practice, the word came down. Leo Boivin, the coach, wouldn't be there. Red Berenson, who was still playing, ran practice.

When I was leaving afterward, I thought I saw my brother leaving the building ahead of me. I went up to see Mr. Francis. I told him, "Leo wasn't down there, and I swear I saw Barc leaving the parking lot."

Barc won a championship the year before at Kansas City as the player-coach, with kids like Brian Sutter and Bernie Federko.

I said, "Is Barc the coach?"

Emile said, "Yeah, Leo's resigning. We're naming Barc the new coach of the Blues."

I was so happy for Barc. I knew this was what he wanted to do. To me, it was just great.

But I told Emile, "I don't want Barc here when I'm not playing great and people are saying, 'He's only on the ice because of his brother.' So I'm retiring again."

Emile said, "The next phone call I was going to make was to you. Your brother's here. We have no coach in Salt Lake City."

They had moved the farm team there from Kansas City.

Emile said, "I'd like you to go down there and be the playing coach. Go home, talk about it with your family."

I did, and I decided that's what I wanted to do.

Behind the Bench

My first game as coach with Salt Lake was in Tulsa. Emile and his assistant GM, Dennis Ball, were both there. We won the game 5-1 or 4-1, something like that, but I was so nervous. I was a smoker at the time, and I pulled my cigarettes out of my pocket during the game and lit up.

Floyd Thomson was playing down there near the end of his career, and he said, "Coach, no smoking on the bench."

He was laughing. All the guys were looking and nudging each other. After that, I always emptied my pockets on my desk before I went on the bench.

With seven seconds left in the second period, Tulsa had a penalty. The faceoff was in their end, so I pulled my goalie for an extra skater. I was thinking seven seconds might be a little long, but they had a man in the penalty box.

Doug Palazzari, who's now executive director of USA Hockey, was my center man out there. He came over and said, "Bob, we've still got seven seconds left. That's a lot of time with an empty net."

I said, "Doug, we've got six players to their four. If you can't win an important faceoff with two extra guys out there, we're going to be in trouble all year.

"Tell the wingers to go for their men and tie them up and run interference. Then we'll have two guys left to get the loose puck."

Well, Doug won the faceoff right back to our defenseman, who took a shot and scored with five seconds left. I'd always wanted to do that, pull the goalie with a few seconds left in a period. I did it in my first game. And it worked.

After we won the game, Emile and Dennis came down to shake my hand. Emile said, "How do you like coaching?"

I said, "I didn't realize hockey players were so stupid till I got behind the bench."

Emile said, "That's just your first game."

I said, "Didn't take me long to figure it out, did it?"

I went out and put an extra case of adult beverages on the bus. Salt Lake was one point out of first place before the game. With the two points for the win, we were a first-place team.

Barc had sent me a telegram before the game saying, "Good luck tonight. Take care of my boys."

The next day, my telegram to Barc was, "I did in one game what you tried to do all year. Put the team in first place."

I had a lot of older players down there like Floyd Thomson who made the job very easy for me. I was the player-coach, but a lot of games I didn't dress.

The Blues did not make the playoffs that year. They were rebuilding, as I said. After their season ended, Salt Lake City was in the Central League playoffs. Barc came down to coach, and I went back to being a player.

It was fun playing for my brother in Salt Lake. Barc was intense. All he asked was that you go out and give it your all. If you lost, it better not be because you weren't trying. Barc was loved by his players everywhere he coached. Try and find one player who didn't like playing for him— you won't.

We lost in the first or second round to the team that eventually won. And then I retired for good.

The First Pro Scout

The next season, 1978-79, Barc was back coaching the Blues. Emile told me the job in Salt Lake was mine if I wanted it, but my family was in St. Louis and I didn't want to move them.

So Emile said, "Come into the office and learn the management side of hockey. Sit in when we're talking to the agents. Visit some of the amateur kids we own the rights to. Watch the farm clubs. We'll keep you busy."

So I started learning all of that. The next year, Barc was in the dressing room by himself and had a seizure. He was banging around and he made it to the phone and called for help. He had bruises all over him and they took him to the hospital.

They did all the tests. What they found was scar tissue on his brain. Barc had been injured playing hockey in the minors with the Ottawa-Hull Canadiens. Scotty was the coach there. Barc got a stick over the head, which left scar tissue.

So Barc was out for a while. Red Berenson took over for the rest of that '79-80 season, and Barc was the assistant when he came back.

After Red took over, he and I sat down with Emile in Emile's office. We had a big part of the schedule coming up, starting with Philadelphia.

Red said, "We don't know anything about these guys. Their lineup has changed since the first time we played them."

There were no satellite dishes at the time. No videotape. No games televised nationally in the States except maybe a game of the week. If you wanted to see a team play, you had to go see it. But nobody did that then. Your GM and assistant GM might see an NHL game other than their own, but only if it was in the area where they were out watching juniors or guys in the minors.

There was no such thing as pre-scouting.

While Red was talking, Emile had the schedules all over his desk for the other teams. Emile said, "Bob, you go into Philadelphia and watch them play. Get their lines, who's killing penalties, who's on the power play, everything you can find."

So I showed up in the press box for the next game there. Jimmy Watson was with Philadelphia then. He said to me, "What are you doing here?"

I said, "We play you in the next few days, so I just came in to watch you play."

It sounds obvious now, but it really was something new then. They didn't have the hockey notebooks that you can buy now, with the rink surface printed on each page. So I just drew a rink on some paper and charted how the Flyers did their breakouts, how their goaltender played the puck behind the net, where everybody set up on special teams.

I started doing it in all the rinks. I'd phone the information in to Emile, then he'd watch when we played the team to check the information I sent.

Emile got to like it, especially when the pre-scoutinng helped us win a game. Which it did. A lot.

Sometimes the team I scouted would get beat bad after I'd seen them, and they'd change everything around. Then after we played them, Emile would call me and say, "Did you really watch that team play? Because everything was different from what you sent us."

So it wasn't perfect.

Sometimes I'd fly back before we played the team. I'd get with Red and put the lines up for the players. Then I'd talk about anything else I found out, like, "Their goaltender leaves the rebound right in front."

If I scouted Toronto and they lost by a big score, I'd tell our guys, "Hey, Toronto wasn't that bad. They had some bad breaks and some bad calls. So don't think this will be an easy game."

Every time I scouted a team that got beat, it was: "Hey, that team wasn't that bad."

I didn't realize I was doing that. At the end of the year we had the team party, and the players started to imitate me. They had some fun with it. That's how I knew I was getting old. We always did that with Scotty Bowman when we played for him, although not to his face!

When I pre-scouted, I also checked on players on other teams who might help the Blues. You think you know a lot about players on other teams because of how they play against you. If they played well, that doesn't always mean you want them on your team. Maybe the guy was bad in the clubhouse or didn't get along with the coach.

And it went the other way, too. Maybe a guy wasn't playing because his coach didn't like him, but he could help another team with a different coach. Those are things you could find out if you talked to people at the other rinks. All pro scouts do that now, too. But that was another thing that was new 25 years ago.

Pretty soon, other teams started doing the advance scouting. It was an advantage. And it was a way to reward a player who had loyalty to the organization. Make him a pro scout.

I was the first one. I know, because I was the only one up there in the press box with the writers. Now every team has two or three pro scouts. And as I like to tell them, all of them owe their jobs to me!

It Plays in Peoria

In August of '90, Joe Micheletti had resigned from the Blues' coaching staff. We needed another assistant. They had been grooming Wayne Thomas, the coach at our top farm club in Peoria. So he was promoted.

I was in the meeting and I thought it was perfect. Wayne deserved it. He knew a lot more about hockey than most coaches, which is why he's now the assistant general manager of the San Jose Sharks.

Somebody in the meeting said, "Bob, we need a coach in Peoria."

I couldn't think of anybody right off hand. Just before training camp like that, it's hard to find a coach who knows the system and the players.

Then Ron Caron, our general manager, and Jack Quinn, the team president, asked me if I'd coach the Rivermen for one year.

Well, my family was here in St. Louis. But I was True Blue and all that. Somebody had to go to Peoria, and I wasn't going to say no. It wasn't that far a drive from St. Louis—about three hours—so I could get home now and then.

So I was back behind the bench again in the minors.

On the Record

Peoria had missed the playoffs the year before, but we had some good young players coming in. It turned out that 20 guys who played for me that year later played in the NHL.

The Blues training camp started first. They made their first cuts, and we got about 12 players sent down to our camp. Then we went out and lost our first four exhibition games.

The Blues were still looking at our best young players. But two days before our season started, the Blues sent down kids like Nelson Emerson, Kelly Chase, Tony Twist and our goalies, Pat Jablonski and Guy Hebert. All of them went on to play with the Blues and other NHL teams. But even with those guys we lost our opener 4-2 at home to Kalamazoo.

So, now we've played five games, counting the exhibitions, and lost them all. After the game, Dave Eminian, the beat writer for the *Peoria Journal-Star*, asked me if I was worried that we'd never win a game.

I said, "No, I'm not worried about the four exhibition games. At these NHL camps, the worst players get cut first and the best players get cut last. So the guys we had in those exhibitions are not the guys we have now. We lost the opener to Kalamazoo, but we were the best team. We out-shot them. If we play like we did tonight, this team will not lose many games."

That statement turned out pretty good. We won our next 18 games, a professional hockey record. And it's still the record. There were no ties in there to break up the streak, because the International Hockey League was using shootouts then. If you were tied after three periods, you played a five-minute overtime. If you were still tied, you had the shootout till somebody won.

Most of the time we played the same way that we did the first night. Maybe we got a little lucky some times. We came back to tie some games and win them in overtime. And we won some games in the shootout.

But I look back, and the streak should have been even longer. We should have won that first game of the season. And the officiating lost the game for us that ended the streak. We had a 3-3 game against Milwaukee, and they scored off a two-line pass that wasn't called.

But that streak took the pressure off the players and me for the rest of the season. And we went on to win the IHL regular-season and playoff championships.

The Lone Ranger

I didn't let on to the players, but I was nervous back there behind the bench at games. And I was even more nervous during the streak.

It was hard because I didn't have an assistant full time. Teddy Hampson, our amateur scouting director, came down for the first half of the streak. Then he had to go back and do his regular job.

Paul MacLean, our East Coast scout, came down three or four times and stayed a week each time. He and Teddy each came down for a playoff series, and so did Patty Ginnell, our top amateur scout in western Canada.

They'd come behind the bench and handle the defense during games. Then they'd put the skates on at practice. Paul was really good on the power play—and still is. He was an assistant for Anaheim when they went to the 2003 Stanley Cup finals.

Teddy, Patty and Paul were all great. We wouldn't have won the playoffs without them. But most of the season I didn't have anyone to talk to on the road except the radio announcer, Norm Ulrich.

What really helped at the start was having Gordie Roberts as my veteran. He came down from St. Louis out of training camp, and his attitude could have been bad. He'd played 15 years as an NHL defenseman and he'd never been in the minors. He started in the old World Hockey Association at age 18.

I told him, "I know it's tough on you. You don't know what'll happen. You could be here a week or you could be here longer. Who knows?"

He was on a one-way contract, meaning he got paid his NHL salary in the minors. So I knew the Blues wouldn't keep him with us all year.

I said, "I don't have an assistant coach. Help me help these kids, and if you get into coaching later on, this could help you."

He not only agreed, he was our best player. He played six games and had eight assists. And he set the example for our kids. Not just the way he controlled the games, but the way he practiced.

I had different drills, but I knew the players had their favorites from other teams they were on. So I'd say, "Today we'll cover getting the puck out of our own end. Anybody have a good drill?"

Gordie would say, "Oh, I've got a couple."

I'd say, "Okay, today you run the drills."

Different guys would take turns. And the whole team worked. To me, when you've got another player yelling at you in practice, you bear down even more. It's not the coach up there all the time, saying the same things.

Hey, when our tough guys—Twister and Chaser—ran a drill, you'd better do it right! And those two guys really knew good skating drills. They'd been bad skaters coming up and they always had to practice that. When someone had a good drill, I put it in our practice book and we'd use it again.

We'd also watch what other teams did and we'd steal that. I'd say, "We're going to do the Fort Wayne breakout now." And we'd use it against them in the game.

I'd have a 45-minute practice. That's all. Practices are the way you play. The players understood it was serious. You're there on time. We had a lot of movement. I'd like to say that we got more out of 45 practice minutes than some teams that went twice as long.

Then I'd blow the whistle and practice was over. I'd say, "Now *this* is where you get ready for the NHL. For 20 minutes, practice what you're not good at."

The guys would go off by themselves or in little groups. The center men would have a bucket of pucks and go practice faceoffs. Some wingers would go with them. And you'd see a winger like Chaser who would be better than the center men at some parts of the ice, like near the boards on his backhand. And you'd use him there in games.

I'd go into the office, take off my skates, get my coffee and go sit in the stands for that last 20 minutes. You'd have to yell from up there every once in a while if somebody was floating around, doing nothing. But mostly the guys were good about it.

Dave Thomlinson, our captain, was someone I fell in love with when I was scouting. He caught my eye at practice. He was always the hardest worker. He wasn't the greatest skater, but he was one of my favorites because of the work ethic.

Sometimes I'd stay on the ice to show some tricks I learned from guys like Doug Harvey…how to tie up a player in front of the net without taking a penalty…how to pull the puck back and slide over a step when a guy went down to block your shot.

We were winning and having fun. And fun off the ice, too, I think. I don't know. I stayed outside the city. I didn't come around looking for the guys, like Scotty Bowman did.

But I did use some of the tricks I'd learned from him.

Psychic Bed Check

In Peoria, our players stayed at the Holiday Inn for training camp and the start of the season. That was before the players knew who made the team so they could go get apartments.

The hotel had a parking garage next to it. The first three floors were reserved for people in the office building next door. So hotel guests could start parking on the fourth floor.

I had stayed at that hotel for years, when I came in to scout or when the Blues had training camp there. I knew how the garage filled up. If you came in at 9 p.m. you might find a spot on the fourth floor. By 10 or 10:30 p.m. you couldn't find a spot until the fifth floor. From 11 o'clock to midnight, you had to go all the way to the sixth floor. Later than 1 or 1:30 in the morning, you were on the roof. Those were the only spots left.

We had a day off early in the season and I drove to St. Louis after practice to see my family. I didn't get back until 2:30 in the morning. Of course, all the floors in the garage were filled, so I had to go up to the roof.

Near the end where I had to park were four cars that belonged to our players.

I shook my head. I knew what happened, but I was glad it happened. They'd find out early in the season that they couldn't pull anything over on the coach.

That morning at practice I had a meeting in the dressing room. I asked David Bruce, "What time did you get in last night?"

"Ten-thirty, coach," he said.

Then it was, "Chaser, what time did you get in?"

"Same as Bruce, about 10:30."

I went all around the room. Nobody had come in later than 11:30, which was curfew. Then I explained the hours of the garage floors, and that I'd seen four of their cars at the far end of the roof.

I said, "Fellas, I know those four cars came in two or three hours after curfew."

I had to be careful what I said next. I didn't want to come down on a player and have him say, "Well, what did you do when you played? I've heard about you."

So I said, "You four guys in the cars after curfew, I've been there and I've done that. In fact, I probably did more than any of you could ever dream of doing. So don't lie to me. Because I know. And I'll find out."

I didn't say the names of the guys on the roof. I didn't need to. The players put their heads down, but they got the little grins on their faces.

I said, "Hey, I know guys like to have a few beers now and then. There's nothing wrong with that. But if you come to the rink and it interferes with your play, then you're hurting your teammates, your owner and your fans. And you had better change."

You've made a point. Now you make a little joke so they'll always remember it.

After practice, I pulled Bruce over where the other guys couldn't hear and said, "I'll go up to you right before the practice tomorrow and ask what time you got in. You say, 'Fifth floor!' Then I'll say, 'Fifth floor, 10:30?' And you say, 'Right on, coach!'"

The next day, that's what we did. The players all got the grins on their faces again and I thought, "That's great!"

It was a reminder. They're grown men. You make your point with a little joke instead of screaming at them.

From then on, you'd hear guys say, "When's curfew tonight, fifth floor or sixth floor?"

The Gameplan

I didn't have many rules in Peoria. We kept it pretty simple.

I told our players, "Scoring is fun. Winning is fun. But to have fun, you've got to work. I don't care what you do in the other team's end. But before you have fun down there, take care of your own end."

I hated cheaters. Guys who sneak up the ice to get a head start on offense. Guys who come part way back to their blue line, waiting for a teammate to get them the puck.

If a guy was up ice when we were on defense, he'd get talked to right on the bench. I'd go over and say, "I hate cheating. You come back to help, and you come all the way back."

We had four of the top six point scorers in the IHL that year: David Bruce, Nelson Emerson, Dave Thomlinson and Michel Mongeau. But, look at their plus-minus, how many goals the team scored or gave up while they were on the ice at even strength. Emerson was plus 54. Bruce was plus 53 in just 60 games played. Mongeau was plus 31.

These were all offensive players. And remember, we got a lot of power-play goals that don't rate a plus because we weren't at even strength.

A lot of times, you see players with a lot of points and you say, "Well, they didn't play defense."

But we led the league in goals-against average.

The top goalie was Dominik Hasek of Indianapolis. He belonged to the Chicago Blackhawks then before he became the best in the world in Buffalo. Hasek let in 2.52 goals per game. Hebert was next at 2.87. And Jablonski was third at 3.00.

So anyone who looked at our scorers knew they were two-way players, offense and defense.

Call-ups

In the minors, the big reward for a coach is when your general manager would call a player up to the

NHL, even though that hurts your hockey team. We had a lot of callups that year in Peoria, but that's the nice part of the job.

That's what you're down there for, developing players for the NHL. And maybe someone thinks the coach is doing a nice job, too, getting the young players ready.

On the streak, we didn't have the same players for all 18 games. We were winning so much and having so much fun, some players would actually feel bad when they got called up. They wanted to be in the NHL but they liked what was going on in Peoria.

With some guys left behind you'd hear, "We're going for the record, and they're calling up players?"

I was glad to hear it, in a way. But I was mad at the players who said it, too.

I said, "Hey, this is the player's dream—to play in the NHL. Would you be crying and moaning if you got called up? Fellas, let's be happy for the guy who went up. Let's hope that he does very well in St. Louis. Then they'll think maybe we have some more players who can play in the NHL."

The other side of that was, sometimes a player came down from the Blues to Peoria for conditioning or to work on something, and he wasn't in the right frame of mind. He was disappointed. He didn't think he should be down in the minors. He was just going through the motions.

That didn't sit well with me or the other players. We didn't want anyone down there who didn't want to play.

One time we got a young defenseman from the Blues. He played in three games with us and was not good in any of them. He didn't work hard in practice. Our other players were not happy with him.

Players in the minors always watch the big club. They know when someone is injured and somebody might be called up. The Blues got an injury on defense, and we had defensemen in Peoria who were playing well. Tom Tilley. Dominic Lavoie. Robbie Robinson. I would have recommended all of them ahead of the guy that was just sent down.

I was praying, "Please do not recall that guy and reward him for being awful."

But the call came: Send that young defenseman back up. He was a physical player. The Blues defenseman who got hurt was a physical guy. Brian Sutter, the Blues coach, needed a guy who played a certain way. And our best guys at that position didn't fit that need.

So we sent the young defenseman back to St. Louis, and that made my job very hard. What could I say? I had told my players all year, "If the Blues need someone, whoever's playing well at that position, that's who I'll recommend."

I also had told the guys that I'd never lie to them. But at practice the next day, I told them a little fib.

They knew who was gone. They were thinking, "It's not fair."

So I said, "Fellas, you see who's missing."

They all nodded.

I said, "I phoned Ron Caron last night and told him, 'We've got a good thing going down here, but we've got a player who's not ready to play here. I'd like you to call him up for some conditioning.' So Ron did me a favor."

They laughed at that.

I said, "Fellas, I don't think it's fair. But things like this will happen in your career."

And the players were good about it. But then it started with them: "Coach, I don't feel too good today. I need to go up to the Blues for some conditioning!"

A Player's Coach

When we won the 18 games straight, the Peoria owner, Bruce Sauers, wanted to get rings for us. Then it was, "Rings or watches?"

I said, "Don't ask me. Ask the players. They're the ones who did it."

And their answer was: "We'll get the watches now…because we'll get the rings at the end of the year."

And that's what they did. We got a very nice watch, which I still have, and we got a ring when we won the playoffs.

I don't know about being a players' coach. But I'd always ask the players on things like that. And I think they appreciated it. But they had a funny way of showing it.

I'd go into the coach's office in the morning to get dressed for practice, and they had cut my skate laces. I knew who it was. Chase and Twist. All the time.

With the little pranks, the dressing room was loose. Just like it was when I played in St. Louis—although we never did anything to the coach when it was Scotty Bowman!

I'd go to practice and blow the whistle, and nothing happened. It would be full of Vaseline. Another time I took the whistle out of my coat pocket, and the pocket was full of shaving cream.

No matter what they did, I never let on that anything happened. We'd be on the ice, and I'd wipe my hand off or wipe the whistle off and just keep going.

Then things started happening to the players.

When the guys would take their showers, they had these big containers of shampoo in there. I started adding peroxide to it. The players who brought their own shampoo were laughing at the other guys: "Are you guys putting something in your hair to make it blond?"

It was taking a while because you're not supposed to rinse it off right away, like they were doing. It eventually would have worked if they took enough showers. But some players went through my desk to do something to me and found the bottles of peroxide. So I never got a completely blond team.

One time, I left the ice early as usual but went into the dressing room instead of my office. I collected all their shoes, tied them all together in knots and taped them in a big ball.

They came in from practice and said, "Okay, who's got the shoes?" I came rolling them all in front of me, like a beach ball. I didn't say anything; I just left it there and went out. They had to cut all the laces to get them apart. So I had plenty of time to escape.

The Shadow of Scotty

I used to tell my players in Peoria, "My door is mostly open!"

A lot of these young guys looked so good at the start of training camp when we were still all up there with the Blues. It takes the veterans a while to get their timing. So in the early scrimmages the young guys would be flying, and you'd say, "Geez, where'd *that* guy come from?"

Then the veterans catch up and the younger guys get sent down to Peoria. It's a big disappointment for some of them. As each one came down, I brought him into the office by himself. I'd get up, walk around and put my finger right on his shoulder blade.

I'd get really serious and say, "You really screwed yourself."

The kid would say, "What? How?"

I'd say, "I saw you up there at Blues training camp. You're pretty good. You've got a lot to work on, and we will. But you really screwed yourself. Because I saw how good you can play. So don't ever tell me, 'This is my best, Coach.'"

During the season, a kid would be playing bad. And I'd tell him, "Don't tell me this is the best you can play. I know you can do better."

Or if a kid thought he should have been called up, I'd say, "Don't pout down here because you're unhappy with the Blues. When you pout and play bad, you're not hurting the Blues. Look at all the scouts here every night. They're not with the Blues, and they're looking for hockey players.

"So impress these other scouts. Go to another team, maybe, and come back and show the Blues they made a mistake by not bringing you up. But if you pout with all these scouts watching you, there goes your chance to play in the NHL."

And then Scotty Bowman came in.

At the start of that '90-91 season, Scotty was player personnel director for the Pittsburgh Penguins. He had left St. Louis and won five Stanley Cups in Montreal. Then he went to Buffalo as coach and general manager. He had some good years there, but he never won the Cup.

So he was with Pittsburgh, and he came to Peoria for one of our first games. About my door being mostly open? I got Scotty to sit in the office with me before the game, and I made sure the door was open then.

The players would walk in and see him. Everyone knew who Scotty was. Then they'd go back and tell the rest of the dressing room who was scouting them that night.

The next game, Scotty was there, too. He asked about Gordie Roberts. I said, "He's our best player. He's a man playing among boys."

A short time later, on October 27, 1990, Pittsburgh got Gordie Roberts from the Blues for an 11th round draft pick. As a coach, the timing couldn't have been better. I knew I wouldn't have Gordie all year anyhow with that one-way contract of his.

But now I could tell the players, "Gordie Roberts came down here after 15 years in the NHL. He'd never played in the minors. He worked every shift he was on the ice.

"Scouts liked the way he played, and now he's in the NHL again. But if he had pouted—and maybe he had a right to—he'd still be here."

And it worked out pretty well for Gordie, too. He went on to win the Stanley Cup that year in Pittsburgh.

Still the Pupil

Sitting there in my office with Scotty, I'd get little tips about coaching.

Before one game, he heard me ask one of the players, "How's your shoulder?" The kid said, "It's a little sore, but I'll give it a try."

When the kid left, Scotty said, "You know what you just did? If the guy has a bad game, you've given him an excuse. He can say he told the coach he didn't feel well. It's not because he played bad, it's because he didn't feel well. So don't ever ask a player how he feels."

I thought about the three years I played for Scotty in St. Louis, and I couldn't remember him ever asking me how I felt. Even if I got knocked out or the doctor had a needle in me for something.

From then on, a guy would get hit and come off the ice holding his arm, and I'd look the other way. I'd let the trainer deal with him. The next shift, I'd tap him on the arm and send him off. If he couldn't go, he'd tell me. But I never asked first.

Goalie Care

I also got a good tip from Glenn Hall. After he retired, he was the goaltending coach for Calgary. Salt Lake City was their farm club after we moved ours to Peoria, and he'd come down to watch the IHL games.

I was playing two goalies, Pat Jablonski and Guy Hebert, switching off every game because they were both very good.

At the morning skate before the game, I just had the goalie stop shots while we ran our drills.

Glenn told me, "You should tell the goalie who's playing that night, 'If you want a lot of shots, take them. If you want a lot of deflections, ask for them. If you want shots from angles, tell the guys. And when you're ready, get off the ice, whether it's two shots or 200 shots. Just be ready for tonight.'

"That way, after the goalie has a bad game you'll never have him say, 'I took 200 shots today at the morning skate and was out there too long.' Let him make the decisions on how he gets ready. Put the pressure on him. That's what they did to me when I played in Chicago."

Be Yourself

I'd been a player. So that's how I tried to coach, knowing how I felt as a player when something happened.

At Peoria, a guy would make a glaring mistake that would cause a goal. He'd come to the bench and wonder how I would react. I'd go down to the player, and everyone was looking at me, and I'd very calmly put my hand on the player's shoulder. I knew that the player knew he made a mistake, and right then he was feeling terrible.

The thing is, players are in the minors to learn. They're going to make mistakes. It's the coach's job to try to correct them.

So I'd say to the player, "You know what happened out there?"

The player said, "Yeah, yeah."

I said, "Hey, if you know what happened, we'll call that a good mistake...*if* you learned from it. But if you keep making the same mistake, then we have a problem."

That's how I coached.

Oh, they'd get yelled at sometimes. And sometimes you threw something, and it might be fake.

I knew Scotty would look for those blowout losses so he could really give it to the guys. We didn't have many of those. We won 58 games, lost 19 and had five shootout losses where we still got a point.

But one time on the road, we gave up three or four goals early in the first period and got beat. The buses we rode had the TV sets, and the players would watch movies. After that game a player got up to put a tape in and I jumped up. I took it out of the VCR and said, "You want to watch a tape? We'll watch this one!"

I put in the game tape, with all the bad goals right there near the beginning. I walked up and down the bus, yelling, "See that? See that?"

It didn't take long to see all the bad goals. Then I went back up to the front and took the tape out and yelled, "*Stop the bus!*"

I think the bus driver had a heart attack, but he slammed on the brakes.

I yelled, "*Open the door!*"

The players were looking at me and wondering. I said, "You know what we're doing with this tape? Here's what we're doing."

And I threw the tape out the door. I said, "That's it. We won't think about that tape again. Now close the door and let's get out of here."

I did these things and I'd wonder: Are they learning?

And then we'd be up a goal late in the game, and I'd hear a player tell the bench, "The coach says dump it in," meaning the clock.

Or I'd hear someone say, "Use that extra guy on the ice," meaning the boards.

Or I'd hear a guy say, "I hope that's a good mistake," when somebody did something stupid.

And I'd know I was getting through to them—without always yelling and screaming.

Peoria Bottom Line

It's amazing how much fun you can have by winning. It doesn't come easy. You go game by game. It's hard work. We had a tough time in the playoffs, with our best players up with the Blues until early in our second round.

I really enjoyed it. I loved coaching the kids. We were champions. But I also knew that Harold Snepsts was in his last year as a player in St. Louis, and management told him that he was coming down to Peoria as head coach.

Hey, when I first took the Peoria job to help the Blues, I told them I'd do it for one season.

When we started the winning streak, the reporters came up to me and said, "You could be Coach of the Year."

I said, "No, I'm coach *for* the year."

As it turned out, I was both!

The Plagers of Kirkland Lake

My father, Gus Plager, had played senior hockey, which was big in Canada back then. There were only six teams in the NHL, so a lot of good hockey players never got a chance. The senior hockey players got the good jobs in the town where they played.

My dad worked in the gold mines in Kirkland Lake as a sample boss. When they did all the blasting, he and his crew tested the rock samples in the assay office.

But then my dad got a skate in the back of the head. He came very, very close to dying. And it kept him from playing hockey again.

He and my mum, Edith, just had the three boys. And the three of us would have scraps at home, upstairs and downstairs. Your fist or your foot would go through the wall, then you'd cut out a hockey picture from the newspaper and hang it over the hole.

People would come over to visit and say, "Oh, the boys are really interested in hockey. The whole wall is full of pictures."

And my Mum would say, "Here's how they're interested. The pictures are all covering holes in the wall."

She knew, because in the winter the draft would come through the house and move the pictures.

After that, whenever Barc and I had an argument, my dad would have us settle it outside. He would shove towels into socks and put them on our hands. Those were our boxing gloves. That was how you settled the argument. If you won, you were right. If you lost, you were wrong. I was always wrong, because I never beat Barc.

Barc was a man when he was still a teenager. He was mature, and he weighed 190 pounds when he went to play juniors at 16. I was two years younger and I was immature— I grew up fast later!—and I only weighed 160 pounds when I was 16.

But I had a younger brother! So when Billy and I had an argument, with the socks coming out, I didn't mind. As many times as Barc beat me, I beat Billy.

I never played with my brother Barc until he got traded to St. Louis that first expansion year. Barc and I became close after that, but we never hung out growing up. We were in different age groups when we first started playing. Being two years apart meant a lot up there. We weren't really close growing up. He had his friends, and they were all his age. I was two years older than Billy, and he had his friends his age.

Barc was a scrapper in the town. And Kirkland Lake was a tough town. He had fights all the time that weren't hockey fights. When Barc was 16, he had a big reputation in town as a tough guy. And he backed it up.

Every Saturday night as kids, we went down to the local dances. Guys would come in from other towns nearby. And there were scraps. Every Saturday night, my brother was challenged.

Barc beat a lot of guys up. Then as I got older and he left town, it was tough on me. Being Barc's brother, I got challenged a lot, too. I had to be tough.

When he played his juvenile hockey at home, I was the stick boy when he was about 15. The next year, 1957, he left home to play Junior A with Quebec in the Quebec major junior hockey league. The Montreal Canadiens owned the team.

After one year in Quebec, Barc was sent to Peterborough in the Ontario Hockey League. The next year, '59, I was drafted first overall by the New York Rangers in the junior draft and went to Guelph, which was also in the OHL.

Sibling Rivals

When Barc left to play junior hockey, he'd send the clippings back to our house. That improved my playing and my dreaming. I was two years younger, and I was going to be better than my brother. And Billy, two years younger than me, was saying the same thing when I went away.

To make it in hockey, you've got to be in the right place at the right time. Barc was the best hockey player in our family, but it took him the longest to get to the NHL. He was in the Montreal system, and they won the Stanley Cup every year.

They'd go to training camp with 200 players hoping to make the team. There was no room. When you win the Stanley Cup, you don't make a lot of changes. There was no free agency then. You didn't leave unless you retired or were traded.

When I made it to junior hockey in the OHL, I got to hate it. Barc was with Peterborough, and they would play Friday in a place like Hamilton. You'd see in the paper that he was in a big scrap.

And then Hamilton would come play us in Guelph. I'd hear, "Oh, yeah, living in your brother's shadow! Are you as tough as your brother?"

Then I'd have to fight the guys Barc fought. I guess their way to get even with Barc was to beat up on me.

You had to be tougher.

Then Barc left and Billy joined the team in Peterborough. That was good for me but bad for Billy. I'd become a pretty good scrapper and body checker. Then when Billy played in Peterborough, the guys I scrapped with would say, "Let's get even with Bob by getting Billy!"

With the fighting, we learned one thing from Barc: "It's not whether you win or lose. It's whether you show up."

Barc was in a lot of scraps. He didn't win them all. But he liked to say, "I always showed up for them all."

Riding the Bench

My first year in Guelph I seldom played. I was too young, and I was there as a learning thing. So I dressed and sat the bench. I would only play the odd time, depending on the score.

One game at home we were losing like 6-1 with about 20 seconds left. We had a defenseman get injured, and Eddie Busch, the coach, tapped me on the shoulder and said, "Get out there."

I skated down to the far end for the faceoff, and when I got there I called time out. I skated all the way back to the bench and Eddie Bush said, "What is it?"

I said loud enough so everyone could hear it, "Did you want me to tie it or win it?"

He just pointed to the dressing room. So I never got to play the 20 seconds. That's just the way I was back then, but I didn't like Eddie Bush. I didn't think he was a very good coach.

Meeting Emile Francis

That first year at Guelph I got up to maybe 165 pounds. When I had my meeting with Eddie Bush after the season, I was told to go home and put on some weight.

I never heard that from a coach again!

That summer, I worked at the gold mine and I did what the coach told me. When I came back to Guelph for training camp, we had a new coach, which made me very happy. It was Emile Francis. He had retired as a goaltender with the New York Rangers.

I went to the hotel in Guelph to meet him. We shook hands and he said, "Bob Plager…" And he found my stats on his desk, which was covered with hockey stuff like the rest of the room.

He said, "You only weighed 160 pounds. You look a lot heavier."

Not bigger, heavier. It wasn't muscle. It was all fat.

I said, "They told me to put on weight."

He said, "What do you weigh now?"

I said, "Two-oh-five."

Emile said, "I guarantee you right now, when you start the season you'll be a lot less."

He always said that if you were honest with him, he'd be honest with you. So I told him I was disappointed I didn't play more the year before.

Emile said, "I want you to get a reputation. Be a little crazy, a little mean, so you get the players thinking about you."

I said, "That's great."

I got in a lot of scraps that year. Players would push me, and I two-handed them with my stick across the legs. As a defenseman, I learned that the area in front of the net is my area, and *nobody* comes in there.

We had two of the top players in Canada on our team, Rod Gilbert and Jean Ratelle, who both went on to the Hall of Fame. Emile told me, "You take care of those kind of guys, and they'll make money for you."

And that's what I did.

Brother Against Brother

My second year of junior, Barc was the heavyweight with the big reputation. I was the crazy guy. And we happened to meet one night in Peterborough.

Barc came down the ice carrying the puck. I was on defense. The whistle blew. I let up. Barc kept coming. His stick caught me and split my lip open. It wasn't a bad cut, just a couple stitches.

But I went up to Barc and he just looked at me. No apology. That made me even madder. My stick and gloves went down and, being a smart fighter, I got the first punch in.

Barc was kind of stunned. I got another punch in before Barc got going. This was our first scrap in a uniform. I don't think he expected us to fight.

After my second punch, Barc didn't care. It was a hockey fight, brother or no brother. We were down by the blueline, open ice. We threw a lot of punches, some landing and some bouncing off the head. Then we grabbed each other and held and pulled on each other's sweater.

Al LeBrun, our heavyweight, came in to break it up. The referee told him to get out of there. Al said, "But they're brothers!"

The referee said, "That's right. And if we get between them, they could both turn on us!"

We got tired, the fight was broken up, and we got sent to the penalty box. In those days both players used the same door to the same box and sat down next to each other. I stepped up to go through, and Barc, who was so mad, pushed me from behind into the box.

I turned around as he was stepping in and punched him in the head again. He got knocked back and stepped onto the ice, and we went at it again. Not as many punches were thrown because we were tired, but Barc just lost it. This was his home rink and I'd shown him up. Twice.

He wanted a piece of me. I'd seen that look when I fought him in the backyard, and it was, "Uh-oh!"

But players stepped in between us. We both got thrown out of the game, and now Barc was really berserk. I went over by our bench to go down the ramp to the dressing room.

Barc was still after me. I looked back with a big grin on my face, which got him madder and madder. The players and officials were trying to restrain him, and they finally turned him around toward his bench.

I jumped back on the ice and poked him in the back of the head. Not real hard, but it peeved him off even more. Then I went down the ramp toward our dressing room. I looked back, and I could see him on the ice by our bench. All of a sudden, he took off.

I knew what he was doing. He went to his bench, left the ice and came down the hallway to continue it. He was swinging his stick and yelling at me.

I said, "Barc, it's over."

I went in our dressing room and closed the door. I could hear him out there. The ushers and other people out there wouldn't let him in, but I was ready in case he got past everyone.

When the game was over, we got on our bus to go back to Guelph. It was a four-hour drive, so first we stopped for some food at this little restaurant-grocery store by the rink.

A lot of the Peterborough players hung out there. But I hadn't seen my brother, which I was glad of. Believe me, I was a little nervous. I'd seen him lose it before. We went inside. Some players from both teams were there. All of a sudden, the place got quiet. Barc had come in.

I thought, "Uh-oh!"

He pointed to a room in the back. My brother was so much tougher than me, but whatever happened in the back, I had to go. If I took a beating, that's the way it was. I had to show up.

Barc closed the door behind us. I didn't know if I should start apologizing, but he talked first. He said, "This is part of the game. Things get carried away sometimes."

Which I was very happy to hear.

Then he said, "How much money do you have?"

I said, "About 20 dollars."

This was just before Christmas. Barc said, "I've got something I want to get Mum. Give me 15 and I'll put in 15 and it'll be from the both of us."

I gave him the money and he said thanks. Then he said, "By the way, I did not hit you with the stick on purpose."

The story was that he heard the whistle, couldn't stop, tried to go around me and the stick just swung up as he tried to turn.

That's not the way I saw it. Or felt it. But then he opened the door, and the whole store was looking at us. Both teams were there. Word had gotten out that the Plagers were in the back room. People were running down the street to see what would happen.

Then Barc left and I left.

Peterborough was coming to our building a week or so later, and everyone wanted to know if the Plagers would go at it again. That scrap was really written up in the papers in both towns. They had headlines like, "It'll Be Settled in Family Court."

But my brother got hurt in the first period and had to leave the game. Nothing probably would have happened anyway. It was over, as far as we were concerned.

A while later, I found out that Emile Francis had phoned my parents up in Kirkland Lake after the game in Peterborough. Emile told my dad, "The boys were in a big scrap with each other at the hockey game tonight."

My dad said, "How big?"

Emile said, "From the ice to the penalty box to the ice to the runway by the dressing rooms."

My dad said, "Did either of them go down?"

Emile said, "No, no, nobody got hurt."

And my dad said, "Well, I've still got another son up here who'll go down there and put them both on their butts!"

Billy was younger, and he was pretty good. But he wasn't that good yet.

Brother Billy

Billy was traded to St. Louis at the end of our first year in '68. He was up with us for parts of the next three years, which was great.

But when he got into trouble on the ice, Barc and I would step in and do the fighting for him.

It bothered Billy. He'd say, "You guys don't have to do that."

We knew he'd fought in juniors, but he was still our younger brother. We felt like we had to look after him.

Until one night in Vancouver.

Billy was down at the other end of the rink, getting ready to fight with Orland Kurtenbach. Barc and I were on the bench. There was no way we could get out there, and I was glad. Kurtenbach was a veteran, one of the heavyweights of the league. He had three or four inches on Billy and a lot more pounds.

The gloves came off. Billy had Orland's sweater, and they started throwing punches. Orland landed a few, but Billy did very good. *Very* good.

Barc and I looked at each other, and we said, "*We've* been going out fighting for *him*?"

Brother Billy: He proved he could take care of himself, on the ice and in the business world. *(Bruce Bennett Studios)*

That was the talk afterward when we were patting him on the back. And Billy said, "I keep telling you, I can handle myself."

After that night, we knew he could.

Billy played nine years in the NHL with Minnesota, St. Louis and Atlanta. When he retired in 1976, he got a job with Quaker Oats back in Peterborough and worked his way up to being a supervisor. He's still there with a great job.

So Billy could take care of himself off the ice, too.

Meeting Noel Picard

In the minors when we played in Barc's city, I'd go over to his house for a meal the night before the game. He'd do the same when he played in my city. And we talked hockey all the time.

So, I heard Noel Picard stories long before I ever met him. He played with Barc in the minors, and Barc would say, "He's the toughest guy I ever saw. Don't go after him, Bob. I'm warning you now."

I told you about the first junior fight I had with Barc. The first pro fight we had started because of Noel. It was in 1963-64 in the old Central League. Barc was with Omaha and I was with St. Paul.

A guy on our team, Teddy Taylor, started to go at it with Noel. And Noel had the advantage, so I went in to get him. Even though Barc had told me about him. It was two against one, so Barc jumped in and grabbed me.

The four of us all rolled around on the ice. It was not a big fight, but I ended up with Barc. When we were going to the penalty box, Barc said, "Don't say anything to Noel in here. He'll kill you."

Again, it was just one penalty box, and we all went in together. Noel went right up to Teddy and me and said, "You two guys have to fight two by one!"

That was Noel's way of saying it, instead of "two against one."

I said, "Hey, don't talk to us unless you learn to speak English!"

Barc jumped between us. He kept saying, "Bob, you don't realize how tough this guy is."

Later on (it might have been the same game), Barc and I did get in a fight on the ice. Punches were thrown. We went down on the ice, and I ended up on Barc. Noel came from behind, put his arm around me and started to drag me backward.

I was still down on the ice, bent over. Barc got up, took two strides and kneed me in the face.

Noel looked at me and said, "I'm sorry. I don't think he do that to you. You're brothers!"

I was hurting too bad, or I'd have said, "Hey, this happens all the time!"

The same year we were in St. Paul in my building, and Barc's team was beating us very badly. Barc was down in front of our net late in the game and there was a scramble. I cross-checked him. He pushed me. Before he knew it, I dropped the gloves and pulled his sweater over his head. I had him bent over, throwing punches down at him. But I was hitting him on his back, not on his head and not real hard.

They pulled us apart and Barc was going crazy.

I said, "Barc, I had to do something for the fans. You didn't get hit hard. They'll go home and they won't talk about how bad we played. They'll talk about how good that fight was between the Plagers."

Barc said, "You're embarrassing me."

That's what got him. He always thought I was hotdogging it. And that time, I was!

But the thing is, and I learned it from him: On the ice, you'd do anything to win. Even if it was against your own brother.

The Plager Way

When Barc got to St. Louis in the middle of that first year, that's when I really got to know him. Billy came in the next year, and Barc was the example for us. We learned from him: "Your name is Plager. We show up every time. We battle. We play to the end. We play injured. We don't cheat people."

I was the jokester off the ice. On the ice, if Barc thought I was going a little too far in not being serious, he'd say, "That's not the way the game is played." And I knew to quit joking.

We played another game in Vancouver where Billy threw a body check, and a skate came down and caught him in the back of the head. He went down and wasn't moving. It was scary. He was out cold.

Barc and I went out with the trainer. They called for a stretcher, they started to wheel him off to the medical room, and Billy moved a little.

We went back on the bench. A few minutes later we heard, "Move down." It was Billy.

I thought, "Boy, this kid is tough."

But Barc said to Billy, "You just got carried off on a stretcher, and here you're back on the bench?"

Billy nodded.

Barc said, "You embarrassed us. Don't *ever* do that again. If you're not hurt bad, you don't go off on a stretcher. If you do, it had better be serious. And you don't come back in the game."

Barc gave it to him again after the game: "You're a Plager, you don't do that."

Later in that season, we were playing in St. Louis and Billy crashed into the boards in the corner, feet first. The trainer was out there. It was Billy's leg or ankle. He couldn't stand up. They called for the stretcher and they carried him off again.

Barc was standing by the door at the end of the rink when they wheeled Billy off. Billy was in pain, and all Barc said was, "It had better be broken!"

Billy went to the hospital for x-rays. After the game, we were in the dressing room and Billy came in. On crutches. With a cast on his leg. With a smile.

Billy said, "It's broken, Barc, it's broken!"

He was the only guy I've ever seen who was happy to be on crutches. Because with Barc, his leg might have been broken afterward if it wasn't broken then.

Paying the Price

I don't think there has been a player who sacrificed his body more than Barc. And it wasn't a big body. He'd block shots, and his body would be black and blue after the game. He'd have cortisone shots and ice packs,

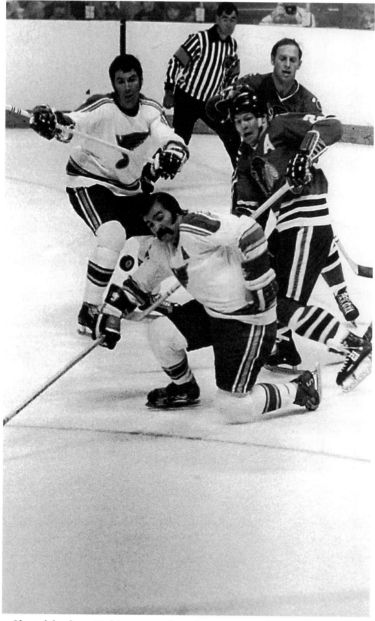

Shot blocker: Taking one for the team, with Noel Picard covering my back as usual. *(Bruce Bennett Studios)*

but he'd play all the games. He never came out. He never complained. And he showed up for practices.

He was our captain on the Blues from '72 to '76, but he was always a leader. When challenged, he never backed down. He would go at the drop of a hat. I'd say, "Barc, it's the end of your shift. The other guy just came on. You're tired. He's fresh. Pick your spots."

That was not his way. If he was challenged, he was going now.

"I don't win 'em all," he'd keep saying, "but I show up for every one."

I saw my brother Barc got his nose broken 13, 14 times. I saw him go to the dressing room and they stuck two pencils up his nostrils. I don't know why, but somehow they'd use them to straighten his nose out.

His nose got broken so bad one time he had to wear a mask. I have it at home. It looks like a little goalie mask. But he kept playing.

Brothers, not Partners

Barc and I were both left-handed defensemen. Barc usually played with Al Arbour, a left-handed defenseman who was better on the right side. I played with Noel, who was right-handed.

Barc and I played the same way. When somebody broke in, we played the puck carrier and hit him. If the guy shot the puck in, our partners would go get it.

Barc and I didn't play well together. I couldn't play the right side, and Barc had a hard time over there, too. Sometimes, Scotty Bowman had us kill penalties together if our partners were in the penalty box. And we took a few odd shifts together at even strength. But when a guy shot the puck in, both of us would step up to take the player.

Barc would say, "It's your job to get the puck."

I'd say, "No, it's your job."

We'd argue all the way back to the bench. One time, we came back and Barc was all wound up at me. He slammed the door and kicked the boards.

A couple shifts later, Scotty said, "You're up, Barc."

We weren't going out together, and Barc said to me, "You go."

I said, "He called you, not me."

Barc said, "I can't go. Look!"

When he kicked the boards, his skate blade got stuck and he couldn't move it.

Oh, Brother

I knew which buttons of Barc's to push. There's that picture of the two of us, skating alongside each other by the net that was really popular. It's hanging in a lot of bars in St. Louis. We'd see the picture some place, and somebody in the bar would say, "Great picture!"

I'd always say, "Yeah, except Barc's out of position."

Barc would say, "I am *not!*"

I'd say, "Hey, I'm left defense. And you're standing right next to me."

He'd say, "They shot the puck around and I had to go get it!"

This went on for years and years.

I finally said, "Barc, you know when I say you're out of position?"

Right away he said, "I was *not* out of position!"

Brotherly partners: The popular photo—at least with me—that shows Barc and me, with Barc obviously out of position. *(Bruce Bennett Studios)*

I said, "Barc, haven't you figured it out yet? We're both on the same side. We're both left defensemen. I don't know which one of us was supposed to be on that side. It could be either of us. I'm just saying that to pull your leg and get you going. And it works every time."

He got that little grin of his. Now he was happy.

Then I said, "Oh, by the way, you *were* the guy on the wrong side."

And it started all over again.

The Babysitter

B arc was the best babysitter in hockey. My brother worried about me more than anybody.

In the middle of summer, Barc would say, "How's your weight? You've got to get in shape. Let's play tennis. You've got to do this."

I'd say, "Don't worry, it'll be all right."

Barc would say, "No, we've got to get going. Now!"

In St. Louis, Barc spent the whole first year in the same apartment building as me, just down the hall. Our second year down here in St. Louis, I was in the team hotel for camp. Barc would say, "You've got to go get a place. Come on. After lunch, you're coming with me."

Then he'd drive me to the area where he and Helen lived and say, "Here's the apartment. It's furnished. Here's the key."

As he moved, I would move.

My brother Billy was good friends with Terry Crisp, and they lived together in the Georgetown Apartments.

I was by myself. So Barc worried about me. And I gave him plenty to worry about.

My First Agent

Years ago, players didn't sign long-term contracts. We signed year by year. There were no agents. We took what the team offered us or we didn't play. We were always treated fair by the Salomons. We had our playoff money, and bonuses for shutouts and goals-against average.

But we went to the Stanley Cup finals our first three years. When it was time to do our contracts with young Sid, Barc said, "I'm going to tell them what I want."

I said, "Good luck!"

I was going in right after him. Barc was just in there a short time, and he came out with a big smile.

He said, "I got more than I wanted."

I said, "How much?"

He said, "Not money. I got a one-way contract."

Mind you, he got the raise that we were all going to get. But here was a guy with a family who rode the buses for almost six years in the minor leagues. The one-way contract was a big thing. If he got sent to the minors, he still got paid his NHL salary.

And Barc was told, "You earned it."

Then it was my turn. I hated to go in and argue. So I decided to have Barc go in with me.

I said, "Sid, I'm not talking to you this year. I've got an agent."

Which was unheard of.

I told Barc, "Go talk to Sid."

So they went into Sid's office. A while later, Barc came out and Sid told me to come in. He said, "Here is what your agent and I settled on."

He showed me the contract, which was way below what I thought I should get.

I said, "I'm not signing that."

Sid said, "You have to. Your agent agreed to it, and he represents you."

I said, "Wait a minute." I called Barc in and told him, "You're fired!"

Then I sat down with Sid and got the contract I wanted. Or at least more than my agent got me.

Barc the Coach

In '76-77 Barc went down to Kansas City, which was the top Blues farm club, as player-coach. That was the last year that the Salomons owned the team. It was the last year that I played. And it was a very good year for Barc.

He'd never coached before, but Kansas City won the regular-season championship and went to the playoff finals and won that, too. Barc was also voted the most valuable player of the league at age 36.

People would say, "Boy, that Barclay Plager is something!"

But that's what you expected from him.

The Blues even recalled him for a few days that year. I don't know if he recommended himself. But he played two games and got one assist.

Barc, Bernie and Brian

B arc got a couple of young guys down there that year in Kansas City, Bernie Federko and Brian Sutter, our top two draft choices in 1976. Bernie Federko had a bad ankle in camp and couldn't really show what he could do. Brian Sutter was a little Barclay Plager, he worked and he banged. They became very close to Barc the rest of his life.

Whenever Barc talked to managment, he would say, "Hey, I've got a couple kids down here who will be in St. Louis before the end of the year. But you don't bring them up one at a time. They have to come up together because they're even better on the same line."

When they came to St. Louis, which they did that season, they brought a lot to the team. They came up with

Barc's boys: My brother was right when he said Bernie Federko (24) and Brian Sutter (right) were best when kept together. *(Bruce Bennett Studios)*

another young guy, Rick Bourbonnais, and the three of them were The Kid Line.

But there was no money in the organization at all. One time during the season, they ran out of hockey sticks in Kansas City. Whenever they had a fight, and all the sticks and gloves were all over the ice, Barc had a designated guy go out and steal the other team's sticks.

Any player he sent up to the Blues during the season went up with only two sticks—and had to come back with a dozen.

Bad News

B arc took over as head coach of the Blues the next season, in February of '78. But Barc was only the head coach until December of the next season.

What happened was, I was scouting down in Dallas one night and I got a phone call from Emile Francis, the general manager. He said that Barc had suffered seizures and was in the hospital. They did the CAT scan and all the tests, and they discovered the scar tissue on his brain.

Emile made Red Berenson, Barc's assistant, the head coach. They put Barc on medication. He would still have seizures, but less and less. So he went back as Red's assistant.

I was with Barc one time when he had another seizure. I had to promise not to tell anybody on the team. But I did have to tell the doctors. They changed his medication, and for years it never bothered him again.

Red stayed the head coach and Barc the assistant coach until March of '82. Then Emile let Red go and took over the team with Barc still as the assistant. Then Emile made Barc the head coach again in December of '82.

But after that season, in the summer of '83, Harry Ornest bought the team. Harry brought in Jack Quinn as president. They hired Ron Caron as general manager, and Ron hired Jacques Demers as head coach.

Barc and I didn't know whether we would have jobs with the Blues until the start of training camp. We both had offers to leave the Blues. But Barc kept saying, "Just wait. Things will work out."

And he was right. They wanted Barc to assist Jacques, and they wanted me to keep scouting. But you didn't make much money with Harry Ornest. He was paying Jacques $50,000 as head coach. I don't want to tell you what I was making—it was so ridiculous. I never knew what my brother made.

We had the smallest hockey staff in the league. Teddy Hampson did the amateur scouting with Jack Evans and Patty Ginnell. I did the pro scouting, and there was Ron, Jacques and Barc. Norm Mackie was the trainer, and Frankie Burns was the equipment manager.

That was our hockey staff. And we were all very close.

Things went on that year because Harry wouldn't spend any money. But we had pretty good players, and they understood what was going on. And Jacques was very good with the players.

I was the go-between for everybody.

Ron would say to me, "Bob, you go tell Harry this," and "You go tell Jacques that!"

Jacques would say, "Bob, you go tell Ron this."

I was in the best shape of my life, running from Ron's office to the coach's office and back upstairs.

There were many nights that Barc and Jacques and I sat around and shook our heads. What made it easier for Barc and Jacques that first year of Harry's regime was the players: Brian Sutter, Rob Ramage, Bernie Federko, Mike Liut, Joey Mullen, Wayne Babich, Jorgen Pettersson.

And Barc had his favorites: Tim Bothwell, Terry Johnson, Mark Reeds. And Rick Heinz, the little backup goalie, was a fan favorite.

No matter what was going on with Harry and the financial stuff, you had better play your butt off. Brian and Rob and Bernie made sure of that. Mike Liut made sure that if you scored on him in practice, you had to earn it.

Jacques relied on these guys and used these guys. And these guys would do anything for Barc. It made for maybe not the greatest team, but they worked all the time.

The second year of Harry's regime, they added Doug Gilmour, who was an exciting young player. Harry traded Liut, which was tough on the team, but Greg Millen came in and played super. Ron Caron brought in Doug Wickenheiser and the quiet guy, Greg Paslawski, from Montreal.

The Worst News

This is the kind of person Barc was. And how strong he was.

I got another call late in '84, the second year with Harry, that Barc was in the hospital. I went to see him, and his wife Helen was there.

And Barc said, very calmly, "They found something in the back of my skull. It's a tumor."

I heard that, and I got up and walked out of the room for a couple minutes. It was hard to take. It's still hard to think about.

What if? Bad seizures and bad timing kept Barc from establishing himself as an NHL head coach. *(Bruce Bennett Studios)*

I went back in the room and Barc said, "Hey, Helen and I talked it over, and we're going to battle it. And we'll beat it."

The media knew that Barc was in the hospital, but nothing was brought out right away about what he had. There was a game that night, and Jacques coached by himself. We didn't tell Jacques and Ron and the players until after the game.

This is how great Ron Caron is, when it's tough and you need a friend. Ron and I went off somewhere during the game and I told him about Barc. We sat and I did my crying. And Ron was very, very positive.

After the game I told Jacques and he took it well. It was tough because Barc and Jacques were very, very close. They were the whole coaching staff, and Jacques really relied on Barc. They went out together all the time on the road.

But then we found out that the tumor was inoperable. Barc and Helen phoned my parents, and then the radiation started.

Showing Up

Barc kept saying, "This is something we're going to beat."

But he knew the odds were not good. He just said, "If this radiation doesn't work, we'll find something else to try."

The doctors told Barc that with the radiation he was going to change. His body, his hair, his energy. There were some tough days there while he got the treatments, but he was always there at the rink afterward. Some days he wasn't himself. The players knew on those days, "Just leave Barc alone."

But the doctors told the players that if Barc saw anybody feeling sorry for him, he'd be the first to say, "I'm bothering the players. I'll stop coming to the rink."

The doctors didn't want that. Coaching was motivation for him to fight the tumor. So they told the players, "Don't feel sorry for him. That's the last thing he wants. Treat him like you always do."

So there were some little jokes, by the team and by Barc.

Barc got a toupee when his hair fell out. He called it "the rug." We practiced at the Affton ice rink then, and it was really cold. One time someone asked Barc, "Isn't it too cold for you to be out there?"

And Barc said, "It's okay. The rug's insulated."

Another time, Frankie Burns, the equipment manager, was vacuuming the dressing room at The Arena. He looked into the coaches' office and said, "Barc, I'm vacuuming the rugs. You want to throw yours out here?"

Lotto Trouble

Not every joke turned out the way it was supposed to.

Barc and Jacques would play the Missouri Lotto together. It wasn't $200 million dollars like the Powerball is now, but it was three or four million bucks. They would spend like $10 on tickets and pool them in the desk drawer in the coach's office at The Arena.

Right before the hockey game on Saturday night, the state would have the Lotto drawing live on KMOX radio. Frankie Burns would listen to the radio in the equipment room, copy down the numbers and bring them to the office. Jacques would take out their tickets. And before he'd look at the numbers that Frankie brought in, Jacques would always say: "Barc, this could be it! This could be the night we finally say, 'Harry, we're out of here. It's all yours— we're gone!'"

Then they would check the numbers. And Jacques would say, "Barc, we work tonight."

One Saturday night, I slipped into the office, took one of the tickets they'd bought and copied down the numbers. When Frankie got the real numbers, I gave him the numbers that I had copied. I told him to write those numbers on a different sheet of paper and hand them to Jacques.

My brother was sick and sitting in the chair kind of hunched over. I thought this prank would cheer him up.

Jacques stood up and started his usual speech about, "This could be the night…" He was about four feet from the wall behind him. Frankie gave him the numbers that I had copied, and Jacques was comparing them to each of the tickets they bought. Every time it didn't match, he said, "Well, Barc, it looks like we're working tonight."

On about the fourth one, the color was changing on Jacques' face. He fell back against the wall and said, "Barc!"

And Barc said, "Jacques, don't you joke with me, I'll punch you right in the face!"

Jacques said, "Barc, I'm not joking."

Barc was getting white, and he started shaking, and he said, "Jacques, I'm telling you, don't joke with me!"

Jacques's legs started to go out, and he was sliding down the wall toward the floor. He said, "Barc, I'm not kidding!"

Barc was sitting there, and he looked like he couldn't breathe.

Suddenly, what I thought was something that would be pretty funny was turning into two guys almost having heart attacks.

So I had to say, "Guys, those aren't the real numbers. I was just joking. Here are the real numbers."

Then Frankie got out of there. And I was right behind him.

My brother finally came out and found me and said, "If you ever do that again, I'll kill you!"

Jacques was very close to Frankie, who had a lot of health problems. Jacques was very good to him. And Jacques came after Frankie and said, "I never thought you would do that to me."

And Frankie would say, "It wasn't me. It was Bobby. He's the one who got the numbers and made me write them down."

Then Frankie came to me, all upset. I said, "Just tell Jacques that at least he was a millionaire for about five seconds."

It took a long time for Barc and Jacques to get over that. And *they* weren't joking. That was a genuine mad.

It's funnier now than it was then. Of course, when they finally did cool off, every once in awhile I'd say, "Hey, you two got your Lotto tickets this week?"

Pinch-coaching

B arc had to miss some time being sick. We talked about getting another assistant coach, because Barc was worried about Jacques not having any help.

I said, "Jacques, if we bring someone else in, Barc might think we don't need him. Why don't I fill in for him while he's sick? Then he can coach whenever he feels up to it."

Jacques thought that was great. And then I could say, "Barc, these guys are driving me crazy. I've got to get back on the road and start scouting again."

And Barc would tell Helen, "I've got to get back down there. They need me."

The thinker: I usually let Jacques Demers (standing in background) do the talking when I (standing in front) would pinch-hit for Barc as the assistant coach. *(Bruce Bennett Studios)*

Plan B

Brian Sutter and Rob Ramage and Bernie Federko would pick Barc up at home, drive him down to the rink and work with him on the machines when he did his rehab.

But the radiation didn't work and the chemo didn't work. The cancer was inoperable. What else could the doctors do?

A new experimental treatment.

They realized that there was not much chance of it working. But it could give Barc some more time in the short run, and in the long run it could help somebody else by leading to a cure. And that's what Barc wanted to do. So I went back behind the bench, and Barc underwent the treatments.

They put steel rods down into the tumor and put heat into it for I don't know how many hours. Barc's right side would be paralyzed afterward, and he went through a lot of pain.

But the tumor was getting smaller.

He was at St. Luke's Hospital in suburban St. Louis. There was always a Plager in the waiting room—Helen and one of their kids—Kelly, Karen, Kevin and Karri—or myself.

I told Helen, "You are one strong person to deal with what you're going through. I think I've cried more than you have."

She said, "I have a little crying room downstairs. When there's nobody home, I go down there and close the door and ask why. But when I leave and close the door, that's it. No more crying."

Barc the Spark

When Barc was getting his experimental treatment, Brian, Rammer and Bernie—our three captains—would go up to the hospital to see him after every game.

That '85-86 season was sort of dedicated to Barc. And he came back behind the bench for the last part of the season and the playoffs.

My brother's banner with his No. 8 on it hung up in The Arena, since the Blues had retired it years before. When our players went on the ice for warmups, they all looked up at the banner with that "8" on it. That became the inspiration.

They saw what he went through, and he never complained once. You have to believe you're going to win every hockey game. And he believed he would win with the cancer.

They played for the team, but those playoffs they were also playing for Barclay. And they had better play hard, or those captains would grab them.

One time we had a player in the medical room, ice packs on a charley horse, who didn't know if he could play the next game. Barc was in the back of that room because his shoulder was sore. He was getting a shot of cortisone so he could make it through the game behind the bench.

Brian Sutter saw that. And when the player came out, Brian grabbed him and pointed at Barc way in the back and said, "Look what he's going through. He'll be here the next game."

And so was the player with the charley horse.

Miracle Monday

I don't know if we over-achieved in those '86 playoffs. We had some pretty good players but not a lot of depth. Harry made Ron trade Joey Mullen to Calgary. And there we were in the conference finals against Calgary, a team that was so strong.

We were down three games to two. We came back to The Arena on a Monday for Game 6. If we lost, the series was over.

We were down by three goals in the third period. I don't know what was said to the guys after the second period, but we picked it up pretty well. Brian and Bernie played great. Greg Paslawski, one of Barc's favorite guys, got the tying goal, and Doug Wickenheiser, another of Barc's favorites, got the overtime winner.

We were on our way to Calgary for Game 7. If we won, we were in the Stanley Cup finals. Calgary was the better team, but we had something special to get as far as we did.

It was Barclay Plager.

Game 7 was a 2-1 hockey game and we lost. Everyone was proud of what the team had done. But I went down to the back room of the Saddledome where Barc and Jacques were, and we kept saying, "One goal from the Stanley Cup finals…one goal."

Then the players started coming in one by one.

Bernie came in and gave Barc a little hug and said, "Sorry, Barc."

And Barc said, "Hey, it's okay. We had a heck of a year."

Brian came in and said, "Sorry, Barc."

And Barc said, "Hey, don't worry. We had a great run."

Rammer came in, same thing: "Geez, Barc, I'm sorry."

He had the tears. And Barc said, "Hey, have you guys found an X-ray I haven't seen?"

But he knew they all wanted to win the Cup for him. Nobody knew if he'd have another chance.

A Hard Goodbye

The next season, 1986-87, Jacques Demers went to Detroit. Ron Caron hired two young guys, Jacques Martin as head coach and Doug MacLean as a second assistant. Barclay wanted to help break them in, but he was too sick to work every game. I had to fill in for him.

The next year, '87-88, Barc was obviously too sick. Ron hired Joe Micheletti as an assistant, and I went back to scouting.

Barc kept getting weaker. After the holidays, he went to the hospital for good. There were some promises made to the dad by the four kids. Karri, the youngest, said she would come back to St. Luke's and be a nurse when she grew up. She wanted to help other people, like they had helped her dad.

Brian and Bernie and Rammer showed up after every game and sat there in the room with Barc. His eyes were open, but the doctors didn't think he was conscious. The guys did. They would sit and tell stories about the game. I really believe that he could hear them.

My dad never could bring himself to come down and see Barc when he had the tumor. It was too hard on my dad. He would send our Mum down. It took a lot out of my dad, and he died a year or so after Barc got sick.

When Barc went into his coma, I told Mum, "Barc's waiting for the All-Star game. All his friends will be in town."

Barc and I were honorary captains for one conference. Al Arbour was honorary captain for the other conference. We were supposed to go to center ice to drop the puck before the game.

Barc died on February 6, 1988, three days before the All-Star game.

We went to the funeral home the day of the game, and that night we had a police escort to the game.

Mum said, "Barc must have been pretty good here to have all this done for him."

Rob Ramage was on the All-Star team. The honorary captains came out for the opening faceoff: Al, Barc's two boys, Kelly and Kevin, and me. Wayne Gretzky gave me my All-Star sweater. And Rammer, who always gave Barc credit for making him an All-Star, gave Barc's sweater to his two boys.

Then the fans started chanting, "Bar-clay, Bar-clay, Bar-clay."

Barc's friends came the next day to the funeral. Every team had players representing them. Scotty Bowman, who left here and coached the Montreal Canadiens to five Stanley Cups, was there. Al Arbour, who left here and coached the New York Islanders to four Stanley Cups, was there.

By the way, the promises made by Barc's kids were kept. Especially by Karri, the youngest. She's now married with two kids. And a nurse. At St. Luke's Hospital.

The cancer was supposed to beat Barc in less than a year.

My brother "showed up" for 40 months.

Barc and "Harold"

When Barc and I would be out eating lunch, sometimes he would say, "This is probably a good night for Harold." That's what he called himself when he went out with the boys. It wasn't Barc going out. It was Harold.

But in the morning it'd be Barc who suffered at practice. Someone would say, "Geez, Barc, were you really going last night!"

And Barc would say, "Hey, Harold might have been doing something, but not Barc!"

Our favorite place was the restaurant Jackie Smith owned at Highway 40 and Clayton Road. That was our hangout. Because of Jackie, the great tight end, all the other football Cardinals would be there. All of the hockey players got along great with those guys: Dan Dierdorf, Bob Young, Conrad Dobler—all of them.

Our spot was in the corner. Barc always sat in the same chair. Harold's chair.

After Barc's funeral, Jimmy Roberts and Noel Picard and I all went back to that restaurant. Jackie didn't own it anymore. It was our first time back there together in years.

Barc's chair stayed empty. We had a few drinks for Barc and a few for Harold. We had some tears and a lot of memories, a lot of stories. It was emotional for all of us, but especially Noel. He tears up easily.

The place was crowded. All the tables were taken. People were standing. Then somebody came up to sit in the extra chair at our table.

Noel said, "What are you doing, my friend?"

The guy said, "I just saw this chair that nobody's using."

Noel said, "Oh, there's somebody using it, my friend. You might not see him, but there is somebody sitting in it."

One of the
Barclay Brothers

When we all played for the Blues, the score really meant nothing. Some nights you had bad games. But you never took a night off. The people who paid their money to see us always appreciated that.

Again, Barc was instrumental in setting that example. He touched a lot of players, and he touched a lot of fans.

People see me now and sometimes they say, "Hey, you're one of the Barclay brothers!" Some people even call me Barc. I never correct them. If they realize it, they say, "Oh, I'm sorry."

I say, "If you called me something else, I might be mad. But if you call me Barc, there's no reason to apologize."

Coach of the Blues

In the summer of 1992, Jack Quinn and Ron Caron asked me to replace Brian Sutter as head coach of the Blues. I guess most people would be excited.

I said, "Don't do this to me!"

I didn't want to take Brian Sutter's job. He was a friend, and he'd been so close to Barc.

But Jack Quinn said, "Brian Sutter no longer has a job, whether you replace him or not."

This was something the management wanted, not me. You're true Blue, so you do what they ask you to do. Especially since it didn't affect what happened to Brian.

And after I thought about it, I was looking forward to it. Wayne Thomas would be my assistant and do all the technical work, which he was excellent at. Harold Snepsts would be there as the other assistant. He'd be good with the players because he just quit playing a couple years before. I also had Bob Berry upstairs as assistant general manager to Ron Caron. Bob had coached three NHL teams and could really help me.

But I'd watched the game with some of our people upstairs, and I knew exactly what they thought about certain players and how they should be played.

So that was a problem.

We also had three Russian players who joined our team that training camp. Nobody really knew them or what they could do. Teddy Hampson had scouted them a couple times. He thought the youngest one, Igor Korolev, could be a pretty good player but wasn't ready yet. The other two, Vitali Karamnov and Vitali Prokhorov—Big V and Little V—signed big one-way contracts. For that money, they were going to St. Louis no matter what they did in camp.

It was tough for a player to accept that, "Hey, my friends are leaving because these Russians were given a job."

I knew that, and I didn't like that. But Jack Quinn wanted them to play. The fans wanted us to go in that direction. We were one of the last NHL teams to sign Russians.

When I benched one of them, word got to me that I was accused by their agent of not liking Russian players. Well, I didn't think they should be here. Not because they were Russians, but because they weren't ready yet. I said right off that as a player years before, you had to earn your job.

I put one line together, Nelson Emerson and Craig Janney and Brendan Shanahan. They played well and the fans loved them. People thought I had trouble with Brett Hull, but I got along with Hullie. In the first game of the year, we beat Minnesota, and in the last few minutes I didn't have Hullie on the ice.

He looked over at me in disgust on the bench. I said, "I'll talk to you inside after the game."

We went in and I said, "Brett, I'm not coaching the game the way I should. If I have you on the ice at the end of the game and look upstairs, my bosses are going to say, 'What's Hullie doing on the ice? He's all offense.' So I'm coaching for the guys upstairs.

"In the last minute, when they pull their goalie, I think the best player to have on the ice is Brett Hull. Who has the best hands in hockey? Brett Hull. Who can get the puck out of his end the best? Brett Hull.

"If we're down a goal in the game and we're killing a penalty, you know for sure you'll be on the ice. Who has a better chance to score short-handed? Brett Hull.

"And I'll tell you what else I'll do. If there's a faceoff in their end with five or six seconds left in a period, you'll be out there. Even if you just finished a shift. You're the guy who can score a fast goal.

"But the people upstairs will question me. So I coach to please them."

Hullie just smiled the way he does and said, "Coach, you really understand the game, too."

Stepping Down

I quit on October 29, 1992. The day before, I had a little meeting upstairs with Jack Quinn and Ron Caron.

I wanted to step down for a lot of reasons.

I hate to lose.

Barc always told me, "Don't bring the game home with you." But we'd lose, and getting in the car afterward I would not be in a good mood. And I'd say something to my two kids that I was sorry for.

It'd be something silly. I'd say, "Where do you want to go to eat?" They'd say, "We don't know."

And I'd say, "You had all night to think of where you want to go. It's up to you. Name a place!"

So coaching was affecting my family. But that was just one of the reasons.

When I was Blues coach, I couldn't be honest with all the players all the time. I couldn't play the team that I wanted.

We had eight defensemen. They all deserved to play. But I had to sit two of them out every day for reasons that I couldn't say. The orders came from upstairs.

Then we traded to bring Lee Norwood back, and we had nine defensemen. A guy like Rick Zombo had to sit out when he should have been playing.

It was so tough that when one of our defensemen got hurt, I'd ask the trainer, "How is he?"

I'd hear, "Well, he could probably play tomorrow."

I'd say, "Did you tell him that?"

The trainer would say, "Well, no."

I'd say, "Then don't. That way he's an easy scratch for me."

Another Kid's Dream

That night before my last game as coach, I went down to Peoria again. There was a player there we'd had for several years, who worked his butt off. He was a big part of our championship team in '91, but he never played a game in the NHL. And he deserved a chance.

I wanted to be there in person to tell him, instead of making a phone call the way you usually do.

So after Peoria's game, I went in to Kevin Miehm and said, "Kevin, tomorrow night you're playing for the St. Louis Blues."

He said, "You're kidding!"

It was worth it to drive the three hours to see the look on his face. You just knew his heart was pumping so fast.

Again, when you put on those skates as a young kid, your dream is to play in the NHL. And Kevin Miehm's dream was going to be answered the next day.

Pupil vs. Teacher

We started out 3-6-1 in our first 10 games. That's when I decided it was time to get out.

The next game was at home against Pittsburgh. Bob Johnson had gotten sick, and Scotty Bowman took over for him behind the bench for Pittsburgh. Pittsburgh hadn't lost in 10 games to start the season. They went on and won the Stanley Cup for the second straight year.

I wanted to coach one game against Scotty. That's why I told Jack Quinn and Ron Caron that this would be my last game.

At the old Arena, the other coaches used to walk on the ice past our bench to get to their bench. Scotty came by before the game, and he had that chin up in the air like always. He gave me that little look of his and a nod and a smile. Well, a little smile.

I nodded and said, "Scotty." That's all that was said between us.

I really wanted to win my last game against him. And we did, 6-4, stopping Scotty's unbeaten streak, too.

Kevin Miehm got a lot of ice time at center, and he played a great game.

Afterward I was having a hard time with my emotions. I knew I had to go in and meet the media. Jack Quinn came down and tried to talk me out of it. He said, "Bob, nobody knows yet."

I said, "No, I wouldn't be comfortable staying on."

Old School, New School

When we played it was, "How lucky we are to be here."

With the players today it's, "How lucky you are to have us."

But that's not the only difference. In the old days, when you scored a goal you didn't jump up and down and high five everybody. You didn't show up the other team.

Minnesota had a guy named Bill Goldsworthy. When he scored he did the "Goldie Shuffle" and started pumping his arm. One time he went around Barc and scored. And boom! He started giving us the Goldie Shuffle. Barc ran him into the boards, put him down on the ice and warned him, "Don't ever, *ever* do that again when I'm on the ice."

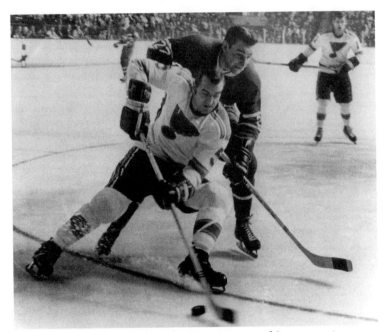

Old school: Montreal's John Ferguson and I saw eye to eye on a lot of things, not just this puck. *(Bruce Bennett Studios)*

Now all the players do that when they score.

John Ferguson Sr., one of the toughest guys in the league with Montreal, never shook hands after a playoff series ended. It's tradition and sportsmanship and all that to skate by and shake hands with everybody on the other team.

My brother Barc never did either, unless we won. Barc would say, "Guys are saying good luck, good luck, and we were just trying to beat each other's brains out? Not me."

When I first came up, you never even talked to a player from another team on the ice. Hey, you'd get fined by your team for that. If a guy did that in Montreal years ago and Fergie saw him, well, I'd hate to be that guy at practice the next day. Fergie would not even play in a golf tournament that other players in the NHL were involved in.

I never even talked to my brother Billy when I got to St. Louis in '67 and he was with Minnesota. And I fought Billy that year in the playoffs, too.

You look at these guys now when they go on the ice for warmups. The teams are on opposite sides of the red line, but the players get close together and they stretch and they talk and they laugh.

It makes me sick. But that's the way the game has changed.

After Barc and I retired from playing, Barc was coaching the Blues and I was scouting. His guys would do something on the ice that was not old school, and I'd say to Barc, "Look, you don't do that!"

And on and on.

Barc would always say, "Bob, I don't like it either. But if we want to stay in the game, we have to change, too."

So I did. But I didn't have to agree with it.

Celebrate the Heroes of Hockey and St. Louis and American Spo

in These Other 2003 Releases from Sports Publishing!

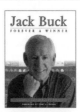